A PICTORIAL HISTORY OF MUSIC

A PICTORIAL

New York · W · W · NORTON & COMPANY · INC ·

HISTORY OF MUSIC

PAUL HENRY LANG
and
OTTO BETTMANN

ISBN 0   393   02107   6

Copyright © 1960 by W. W. Norton & Company, Inc.

Text based on *Music in Western Civilization* by Paul Henry Lang
Copyright 1941 by W. W. Norton & Company, Inc.

Library of Congress Catalog Card No. 60-6822

PRINTED IN THE UNITED STATES OF AMERICA

6 7 8 9 0

CONTENTS

INTRODUCTION

Because I spent my childhood in Leipzig, a city which resounds with echoes of Bach and the entire musical world, I have always had the idea of one day preparing a pictorial history of music. This present book is the result; it combines elements of my professional life as a graphic historian and my private life as a happy lover of music.

A pictorial history of music can never be merely a picture album, however, for no amount of illustrative material can by itself create a meaningful panorama of music. There must be, in addition to pictures, an intrinsic plan, a unified point of view which the reader can grasp and use to achieve comprehension. The history of music which, to my mind, has always been distinguished by just these qualities, is Paul Henry Lang's *Music in Western Civilization*. In an age of specialization, Dr. Lang's book is unique in its broad outlook and vigorous presentation. This book seemed to me pre-eminently suited for adaption as a basic text for a pictorial history of music, and I was delighted to find that Dr. Lang's interest in such a project matched my own.

In condensing and adapting *Music in Western Civilization* I aimed at preserving the continuity of Dr. Lang's text and utilizing wherever possible its broad cultural viewpoint. As for the pictures, I endeavored to illustrate and emphasize those subjects and periods which would be of greatest interest to the reader, and therefore supplemented the chronological sequence of the text at logical points with pictorial, topical, or biographical surveys. Whenever the evolution of a particular school of music or the emergence of a commanding personality demanded more detailed scrutiny, I assembled a picture-text unit that supplements, but does not interrupt, the main narrative.

To give two examples: the discussion of Domenico Scarlatti seemed the appropriate place to complement Dr. Lang's history with a picture unit presenting the rise of the harpsichord. Similarly, the discussion of Richard Wagner was the logical point to survey pictorially his influence on the growth of the orchestra, and the consequent emergence of the modern conductor.

The history of music is a continuous development; and in order to understand and appreciate the more familiar 18th- and 19th-century musical literature, it is necessary to be aware of its roots in the past. Moreover, our musical horizons are expanding today; listeners are learning to enjoy Renaissance madrigals and Baroque choral works, as well as Romantic concertos, and for modern readers, no history of music would be meaningful without a survey of these early periods. As for post-Romantic music, we have provided a detailed coverage of the most recent developments. Dr. Lang has contributed new passages analyzing contemporary music, a task for which he is particularly well equipped both as musicologist and as one of this country's most respected music critics.

All the additional material makes *A Pictorial History of Music* essentially a new book. Its authors hope it will add to the reader's enjoyment of music by giving him a better understanding of how this divine art evolved.

OTTO BETTMANN

Book One

ANTIQUITY

MIDDLE AGES

RENAISSANCE

With his lyre Orpheus charms the wild beasts, the trees, and the rocks. The tragic story of his love for Euridice was used as the subject of many operas.

Apollo and other important gods played the lyre, a privilege they guarded.

Music in the Life of the Greeks

THE CLOSE AFFINITY of the "beautiful" and the "good" was most keenly felt and understood of all civilized nations by ancient Greece. The mere order of these two ideas indicates that the emphasis is on the beautiful, and, indeed, moral precepts often followed and appeared subservient to aesthetic principles. Curiously enough, the Greeks themselves paid much less attention to their plastic genius than to their musical achievements. Classical literature is almost barren of reference to sculpture and architecture, while music is mentioned frequently. There were no muses of the plastic arts. But the protector of music, poetry, and light, Apollo, was the Greek's most beloved God. The charms his lyre wrought upon beasts, trees and stones shows clearly that the Greeks recognized the civilizing influence of music.

Their musical practice centered around the lyre in its two main forms, the lyre proper and its larger variety, the cithara. The lyre consisted of a hollow body, or sound chest, from which protruded two arms curved both outward and forward. The chief wind instrument was the aulos, a reed instrument, not unlike an oboe, or more precisely a pair of oboes. It emitted a shrill, penetrating sound. The lyre was the instrument of the Apollonian cult, the root of lyricism. The aulos belonged to the followers of Dionysus. It was associated with the dionysian rites, its wild dances and dramatic orgies.

A lowly deity like Pan was confined to a wind instrument: Pan playing his flute.

The sound of the aulos was shrill and penetrating. A Grecian girl plays it to entertain a guest.

3

The Dionysian dances, one of the bases of Western drama, moved to the penetrating sound of the aulos. Relief from Myrina.

Closely linked with music and poetry was the dance. This art was found mainly in the drama, the highest expression of the cult of Dionysus. The chorus, while singing its strophes, executed dances which were not mere rhythmical gestures but an elaborate mimetic expression of the ideas in the poem. Aside from this the chorus had vocal functions; it prefaced scenes and accompanied them, expressing the peoples' emotional response to the actions on the stage. However short some of the choruses might be, they formed a considerable portion of the drama. In view of this it is not too bold to say that the artistic impression imparted to the audience in the Greek tragedy was, to a considerable degree, a musical one.

Since music exerted such a marked influence on the mood and spirit of the Hellenes, it could not be left to chance. The state laid down the rules how it was to be performed and applied to the common good. In Athens, Solon was the champion of music. He hoped to promote moral sturdiness and responsible citizenship by musical instruction imparted to the youth. The practice of music was prohibited to slaves, as music was considered a distinctive mark of nobility. Musical education was reserved for free Athenians and the degree of a man's knowledge of music ranked him in the scale of culture. In Greek terms a cultured, distinguished man is synonymous with a musical man.

Scenes in ancient plays were often accompanied by the aulos, which added to the dramatic effect.

4

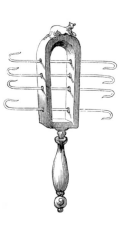

Music was an essential part of Greek education. Solon held that music would give the Athenian youth moral sturdiness and an ordered mind.

A sistrum.

This high esteem also extended to the performers. The Greeks held musical competitions, not unlike the Olympiads, in which the winner was accorded the status of a hero. The pipe virtuoso Midas of Agrigentum was praised by Pindar as a conquering hero, and the trumpet player Herodorus of Megara became a national figure by winning the Olympiad ten times.

To the Greek mind music was part of a mathematical philosophy which the Pythagoreans held to represent the whole of philosophy. Their mathematical theory of harmony was part of a general theory of the harmony of the cosmos, and had its counterpart in the various arts, not only in music. Recent studies have revealed the close connection between the disposition of columns in Greek temples and the elements of the Pythagorean scale.

While the Pythagoreans often drifted into what amounts to number-mysticism, their musical theory followed scholarly precepts of observation, and their conclusions based on the length of strings and number of oscillations form the basis of the modern science of acoustics.

In the transition from the music of antique Greece to that of Christian church, the music of Byzantium played an important role. The original Hebrew songs as sung by the early Christians were displaced by examples of the highest type of antique

musical practice soon after early Christianity came into contact with Greek civilization. Constantinople, after its establishment as capital of the Roman Empire, became the center of a composite civilization, based upon both classical and purely Oriental traditions; but by the sixth century A. D. Byzantine culture and art had crystallized into something definitely divergent from the antique. Byzantine music, based on the music of antiquity, was church music. As such it became an institution closely associated with the destiny of the Church.

Pythagoras, shown in medieval garb, established numerical relationship between the length of a vibrating string and the tone it produces.

5

ten made deacons, even though they might be otherwise simple individuals.

In addition to the psalms, early church music cultivated the hymns, songs of praise, devotion, and thanksgiving. They are the embodiment of Christian devoutness, and have served through the centuries as the musical intermediaries between God and man.

Although the Church gradually approved liturgical singing, it voiced open opposition to the use of instruments whose tones were considered sensuous, "raising impure and voluptuous desires." "We do not need the psalterium, the tuba, drum, and flute, which are liked by those who prepare

Early Middle Ages: The Music of the Church

At its inception, Christianity was not well disposed toward the arts and letters because it saw in them the continuation of pagan civilization. The ancient philosophy of life, with its purely earthly aims, had stressed the sensual power of music. Sensuality however had no place in Christian thinking and at the beginning of the patristic period music was ignored if not suppressed.

Still, music was living all around the organizers of the Church. They had to take cognizance of it. Soon they realized that properly guided music, a most intimate art, a language coming from the very bottom of the soul could very well develop and expand within the framework of the Christian doctrine.

The oldest part of Christian church music was the psalmody, left as a legacy to Christianity by the Hebrew world. Psalm singing was practiced by all strata of society, clergy, people, and children. St. Ambrose held that "Psalms are sweet for every age, and are becoming to each sex. . . they create a great bond of unity when the whole people raise their voices in one choir." When the future pope, Gregory I, was named archdeacon in Rome (585), the appreciation of good singing and the love of a beautiful voice produced a custom which illustrates a high regard for musical ability. People who possessed good voices were of-

Pope Gregory the Great inspired by Holy Ghost (Dove at left) supervises the copying of chants. The collection of Gregorian melodies became the canon of church music all through the Middle Ages.

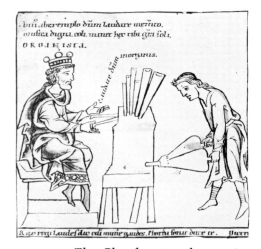

The Church rejected most instruments, but the organ was an exception.

6

themselves for war," said Clement of Alexandria. These restrictions on instruments were reinforced in 590 A. D. when Gregory the Great ascended the papal throne. With all his conviction he excluded worldly elements from the domain of spiritual education, and music, which by ancient tradition formed an essential part of profane learning, undoubtedly came under the same ban. Saint Gregory accepted music only in connection with liturgy. He, and various other popes, organized and codified the many unorganized melodies used by the church singers and established the rules for the solemn chant, which came to be called *Gregorian*.

For centuries Gregorian chant was the only kind of music officially known, taught, and practiced by the Church. From Rome, it was carried all over the Christian world by the ambassadors of the Holy See. As it spread to the west, Gregorian chant came into conflict with the local life, religious rites, and music of the people, and in the struggle it sought to suppress everything else, or at least to assimilate the indigenous, and the secular.

Like Romanesque architecture, Gregorian music unified and fused worldly elements in order to bring them into the service of divine worship. Its beautiful sturdy melodies were the most powerful and effective expression of Romanesque art.

Naturally, Gregory's reforms of Church music took firmest hold in Italy. This circumstance gave Italy for the ensuing centuries a leading organizational position, yet at the same time it retarded the creation of original musical ideas in Italian monasteries. The early Romanesque period produced only one truly important figure, Guido of Arezzo (*ca.* 980–1050).

Guido's achievement, one of the most significant in the history of music, was the organization of a system which still forms the basis of our modern notation. His aim was to educate the singer as rapidly as possible to the point where he would be able to sing unfamiliar melodies by merely looking at the written notation. According to his own statement, a pupil using his method might learn within five months what formerly would have taken him ten years to acquire.

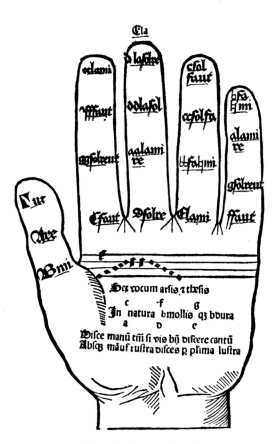

The Guidonian hand was an ingenious aid to sight singing. Guido divided the scale into six tones, the hexachord: Ut, re, mi, fa, sol, *and* la. *The leader of a choir used his hand, so sub-divided, to cue choir boys.*

Guido of Arezzo shows his method of sight singing to Pope John XIX, who was able "to his great astonishment" to sing at sight, without the slightest mistake, a melody unknown to him. (From Hawkins' History of Music, *1776)*

Ladies at the castle sing and dance accompanied by a musician.

The Wordly Songs of the Trouvères and Troubadours

MEN HAVE ALWAYS been fond of singing, and the Church, gradually liberating its strictures, permitted them to borrow her music for purposes not connected with religious worship. The medieval man sang the psalms and canticles in church, and when he departed from service he carried with him the memory of the melodies, which he turned into love songs.

The art of the troubadours descended from the liturgical chant, preserving traditional church scales and even motives of liturgical origin. These carefree wandering minstrels — "no man wot from whence they come nor where they go" — appropriated liturgical melodies for their own use, and as they strolled through France, England,

The jongleurs accompanied their songs with dances and plays. In addition to singing and playing, minstrels recited legends, did acrobatic stunts, and performed magic tricks.

Isolde plays the harp to entertain Tristan. A 15th-century miniature.

A feudal lord has called in his court musician to play him to sleep.

Germany, and Italy, they sowed seeds for the development of European art music.

The chivalric order evolved, according to its needs, a civilization of its own. The heroic, adventurous, and amorous epics of the troubadours appear beside the lives of the saints, and the knight who wrote poetry and sang music offered competition to the learned and devout men of the Church. Courtly love dominated the whole era and imposed its rules both on the art and on the everyday life of the rising social order. The carriers of this new credo were the troubadours of the south and the trouvères of the north.

Troubadour art originated in radiant and sun-drenched Provence; troubadour verses were remarkable for their accomplished artistic craftsmanship. From France troubadour songs spread to Germany, Italy, and Spain. The jongleurs who sang and played their masters' music added a further element; they accompanied their songs with dances and a lively dialogued play.

Meanwhile, the German lands had developed their own brand of lyricism. The German Minnesang mainly created poems expressing the homage (Minnedienst) rendered by the knight to his lady. The Minnesingers remained in many ways medieval men who could not entirely sever themselves from the scholastic tendency of their period. Compared with the spirited, artistic, sensuous, and graceful love lyrics of the French poets, the Germans seem somewhat heavy-footed and angular.

Folk song, artistic minnesong, poetry, and polemic were all united in the sensitive soul of that greatest of German Minnesingers, Walther von der Vogelweide (ca. 1170 –ca. 1230); he gave words to everything that animated his time, wandering from court to court and singing in Bavarian dialect his poems set to music of his own composition.

Poetry and music were fused in the love songs of the Middle Ages. In most cases, the lance-carrying armored knights were both poets and musicians. Their eminently musical chansons accompanied by instruments were at the bottom of certain polyphonic musical forms which arose about 1300 and spread all over Europe.

Walter von der Vogelweide, a chivalric poet-musician.

9

Early Polyphony and the Beginnings of Instrumental Music

EARLY CHRISTIAN CHURCH music was monophonic — that is, it had only a single musical line. Monophony entailed a conception of music which knows only a succession of single tones. The recognition of the existence, beauty, and expressive quality of simultaneously sounding tones, which introduced a vertical as well as a horizontal disposition, resulted in the creation of western music which was fundamentally different from any that had previously been conceived.

The oldest documents of many-voiced music, written in the second half of the 9th century, are called *organa*. Organum was based on a given melody in the tenor, the *cantus firmus* (fixed song or melody), usually a plainchant tune; this was accompanied by another melody which paralleled the first at the interval of the fourth or fifth. Eventually this second melody ceased to parallel the first and achieved a linear design of its own. In these two-voiced compositions we see two melodic lines united in most intimate combination. They appear in parallel motion, then cross each other, then again continue in oblique motion.

The individual parts of organa became increasingly independent: the individual sec-

tions were frequently extended, more than one upper part was added, and these upper parts often were set with completely new texts. The tenor part may preserve the liturgical word (the *mot*) and music as a cantus firmus, while the upper part or parts declaim a paraphrase. These multivoiced songs thus often expressed simultaneously both the original text and commentaries upon it. This type of composition was called a *motet*. The motet was of liturgical origin, but soon found its way into the realm of secular art. There it associated itself with troubadour art and absorbed popular melodies in its polyphonic structure. The result was a remarkably animated and expressive sacred and secular art form.

Instruments also were used in the performance of these vocal compositions. If a singer was not available, an instrumentalist would play his part. Consequently, the instrumental element undoubtedly contributed to the formation of a new musical style. We may go even further and assert that the vocal literature of the 14th and 15th centuries was often performed only by instruments. That this was an acknowledged practice may be seen from the remarks of Guillaume de Machaut, the leading French musician-poet of the 14th century. He held that playing his ballads on the organ, bagpipe, and other instruments was entirely permissible, and indicated that such a choice was part of the performer's right.

Contemporary paintings and literary documents, as well as the descriptions of great marriages and other religious solemnities, reveal the surprisingly rich collection of instruments in general use in the fourteenth century. Viols, harps, psalteries, lutes, hurdy-gurdies, trumpets, drums, chimes, cymbals, bagpipes, reeds, horns, and flutes are a few of the many instruments mentioned. They were all of Oriental origin and were used in a rather monotonous way, excluding all dynamic changes. This same Oriental quality must have prevailed in the nasal falsetto singing which may be clearly identified from a great number of pictures where the physiognomy of the singers is rendered with great accuracy.

Rebec

Lute

Carillon

Horn

Cymbals

Viol

Instrumentalists shown in the collection of religious songs (cantigas) made at the end of the thirteenth century by Alfonso X of León and Castile ("Alfonso the Learned"). This compilation is contained in two richly illustrated volumes now in the Escorial Library. They are one of the most important and valuable documents of medieval music.

11

The great masters of the Flemish school: Guillaume Dufay, who made the Cathedral of Cambrai renowned through all Europe, and Gilles Binchois, who headed musical activities at the Burgundian court of Dijon.

Music and the Burgundian Court

As GOTHIC MUSIC moved toward its apex, the Duchy of Burgundy in eastern France assumed a leading role. Strategically situated at the crossroad of French, Belgian, Flemish, and Germanic influences, the Burgundian musicians achieved a final synthesis of the medieval musical heritage. The productivity of the old Gothic lands had never lagged; and now, enriched by the stimulus of a fresh and joyful art that streamed from the Mediterranean, music burst forth with prodigious vitality.

The leading master of the Burgundian school was Guillaume Dufay (1400-1474).

In the gentle, intimate art of Dufay and his school, a hitherto unknown quality of healthy sensuality is noticeable. A rather plaintive and subdued tone emanates from the music of this age, an age which united the joy of life and religious fervor. Composers of the Dufay period cultivated the song which reflects a perfect picture of the poem which is its text. Heroic and passionate subjects were beyond their reach. Instead, quiet, profound, transcendent feelings were their domain, and self-restraint and tasteful expression their ideal.

Josquin Després was one of the most sensitive and learned contrapuntists of the Burgundian school.

12

The musicians around the aged Dufay confined their activity generally to the north; but the end of the 1470's saw a new exodus of Flemish musicians to Italy, and before long Burgundian music, especially its songs, had rekindled Italian musical art. The Italians embraced the Burgundian style of writing. In turn, the Burgundian singers and composers, attracted by the artistic policies and grandiose liturgical display of the Holy See, the warmth and natural flow of popular Italian music, and the splendor of Renaissance life, flocked to Italy, then returned to the north imbued with the spirit of that seductive peninsula.

Flemish musicians settled in many of the important cities of Europe; these men, who boasted a highly organized musical knowledge and skilled craftsmanship, wrought profound changes in the history of the whole art of music. They prepared the soil of the countries they visited for the growth of Renaissance music, a music which flourished through all classes of society.

Dance in the open. A typical Renaissance scene showing the close link between music and the social life of the period. Painting ascribed to Bonifazio Veronese.

15

Music in Renaissance Culture

An extraordinary vogue of music in the royal and princely courts is noticeable throughout the 15th and 16th centuries. Every important monarch was interested in music, and many of them were capable players, singers, or even composers. When James IV of Scotland came to seek the hand of Princess Margaret Tudor, "he began before her to play of the clavichord and after of the lute, which pleased her very much." The German emperor Maximilian, husband of Mary of Burgundy, founded a court chapel modeled after the Burgundian chapel, and when he traveled he took his large chapel choir with him. Court musicians were considered an essential part of a king's retinue; as a rule, they followed the monarch even in war.

Many contemporary paintings, woodcuts, and drawings attest to the ebullience of musical life in all circles and for all occasions. The enthusiasm for music was not confined to aristocratic circles. In his *Journal du Voyage en Italie*, Montaigne writes that he was "astounded to see these peasants [in Tuscany] with a lute in their hands, and at their side the shepherds reciting Ariosto by heart; but this is what one may see in all of Italy." Luis Milan, the famous Spanish lutenist, described Portugal as being "a sea of music." Every person of culture was expected to be able to take part in an improvised musicale; otherwise he was considered uncouth, and wanting in social grace.

Lutes and viols were the most popular instruments for social music making. Lutes were even made available for waiting gallants in barber shops.

The town bands of German cities enlivened Renaissance festivals with their brassy playing. A mural ascribed to Hans Holbein.

PER NON · ERRARE

Like the visual arts, Renaissance music bases its aesthetics on proportion, relationship, symmetry.

Renaissance instruments were considered either noble or plebian, according to their social acceptability. The bagpipes and reeds were not considered suitable for noblemen. Refined people cultivated stringed instruments, like the lute.

Renaissance theoreticians explored the mathematical basis of music. They strove for proportion, harmony, and clarity.

The Vogue of the Madrigal

THE VOGUE OF social music was chiefly responsible for the flourishing of the madrigal, which came to have an importance far beyond its initial scope as "a short lyrical poem of amatory character." During the 16th century it became the most productive genre of secular Renaissance music.

The first madrigals were written in the early 1530's, and it was not long before they became exceedingly popular. Even serious and severe Church musicians, among

Italian frottolists, serenading their young ladies at carnival time. Florentine woodcut.

them Palestrina, could not escape writing them.

This art form was not, of course, the invention of an individual. One may say, however, that when the first northern composer set an Italian lyric poem to music, the main step toward the creation of the madrigal was accomplished. The madrigal arose in various Italian cities almost at the same time, and its appearance coincided with the height of the influx of Flemish and Franco-

Flemish musicians to Italy. In the final analysis, the madrigal — at least musically — represents an artistically ennobled form of a popular lyric genre, the frottola. Originally frottole were little songs, lively, graceful, and attractive, but ephemeral.

The Netherlanders, accustomed to the skillful combination of several contrapuntal parts, were intrigued by such a free and unconstricted art form. A merger of the two musical conceptions, to which was added the influence of the French chanson, took place in remarkably short time. The madrigal form is one of the most beautiful expressions of humanism; the texts were carefully declaimed, and the meaning was faithfully reflected in the accompanying music.

In no country did the Italian madrigal lead to so brilliant a rejuvenation as in Elizabethan England. Madrigal art started in earnest there in 1588, when Nicholas Yonge (d.1619) edited the first printed collection of Italian madrigals, translating the texts into English. In the dedication to this collection, called *Musica Transalpina,* Yonge speaks of entertaining guests in his house by "furnishing them with Bookes of that kind yeerely sent me out of Italy and other places."

A veritable avalanche of delightful and highly artistic music ensued, produced by a number of important composers. Thomas Morley (1557–1603?), William Byrd (1542/43–1623), Thomas Weelkes (d.1623), and Orlando Gibbons (1583-1625) were among the most eminent English madrigalists. Morley in particular represents a high point in English music. In addition to fine madrigals and canzonets, he was the composer of one or two of the songs written for Shakespeare's plays. He was the most popular composer of his day, and still holds the affection of the modern listener for the light, graceful, and merry tunefulness of his music.

A Renaissance knife carries part of an after-dinner grace.

EARLY ENGLISH KEYBOARD MASTERS

Aside from writing songs the English composers also excelled in pieces for the virginal. In this field England undoubtedly took the lead over the Continental composers. Their excellence is borne out by *Parthenia*, the first printed volume of virginal music published in the British Isles (1611). By far the most remarkable collection of English keyboard music, however, is the so-called *Fitzwilliam Virginal Book*, which contains keyboard pieces by John Bull, William Byrd, and other masters. John Bull was a virtuoso on the clavier, and his brilliant compositions contributed to the growing instrumental literature which Continental musicians, among them Sweelinck, the great Dutch organist, received with obvious pleasure and interest.

An open-air concert of the mid-16th century. Instrumental music of this era was strongly influenced by the popular madrigals.

William Byrd (left), an imposing figure in English Renaissance music. John Bull (center), an outstanding composer for the virginal. Orlando Gibbons (right), keyboard artist and composer of grandiose anthems.

Title page of Parthenia: The Maydenhead *(1611), the first printed virginal collection published in England.*

Orlandus Lassus (sitting at the clavier) and the Bavarian court chapel. From the Mielich Manuscript, Munich.

The Coming of the Counter-Reformation

FLEMISH POLYPHONY and Italian poetry, plus elements of the French chansons, had been fused by the Renaissance musicians into a subtle and appealing art form, the madrigal. This universally accepted genre was ingenious in its musical construction, joyful, and worldly. However, as the 16th century advanced, a new spirit appeared. The Continental composers were swayed by the spiritual upheaval of Catholic Reform, the Counter Reformation, which plunged the Netherlands and France into religious civil war.

Deepening shadows seemed to becloud the arts. Open criticism of, and the prevalent opposition to, secular song was expressed in 1568 by Gabriel Fiamma, canon at the Lateran. "In our language there is an almost infinite amount of poetry, almost all amorous, which fact seems to me quite insupportable and a great mistake. I have therefore redirected Tuscan poetry, in as lofty a manner as possible, toward virtue and toward God."

This conversion from the earthly to the devout and submissive is most clearly illustrated by two figures which stand like guardians at the door leading from the Renaissance to the sombre and often convulsive era of the Baroque. These figures are Orlandus Lassus and Giovanni Pierluigi, called da Palestrina.

Orlandus Lassus, the most versatile composer of the secular 16th century, wrote innumerable chansons before he mended his ways in his later years and turned to poetry that voiced the sentiments of his Church. He began with erotic song and ended with the spiritual madrigal.

Born in 1532 (1530?) in Mons, the territory which gave to music a host of great composers, among them Dufay and Josquin Després, Lassus started his career in the usual manner as a choirboy in his native town. Ferdinand Gonzaga, Viceroy of Sicily and general of the Netherlands armies of Charles V, took the boy with him to Sicily and Milan. After much wandering he assumed the position of choirmaster of the Lateran. In 1560 he settled down at the court of Duke Albrecht V of Bavaria in Munich. With a few years' interruption, he remained in the service of the Bavarian dukes until his death, June 14, 1594.

The works of Lassus, some two thousand compositions, embrace every musical form of his period and show the composer equally at home in all of them. The lovesick complaint of the Italian madrigal, the subtle delicacy of the French chanson, the robust quality of the German part song are each expressed as though from the heart of an Italian, a Frenchman, a German. Furthermore, this Netherlander rose in his Psalms to majestic heights, conveyed in his Masses and other liturgical pieces the serene mood of the liturgy, and spoke in his motets with the voice of one deeply immersed in mysticism. Lassus displayed remarkable literary taste and a sense of humor given to few people. Within the wide range of the forms of his compositions, variety abounds, and one can hardly speak of a "Lassus style" as no two of his works resemble each other. Yet all of his works have one common characteristic: a consummate and miraculous mastery of the technique of musical composition, expressed with equal brilliance in the little popular song forms and the most complicated cantus firmus Mass.

Orlandus Lassus: As a choirmaster "he gave the time so expertly, that like warriors at the sound of the trumpet the singers needed no other orders than his powerful countenance."

Palestrina: A sacred musician who created Masses of seraphic beauty.

His works are a synthesis of two hundred years of musical culture, a synthesis of such convincing strength and plastic beauty that the history of music experienced its like only once again, in the art of Mozart.

In his life work Palestrina proved that polyphonic music, the creation of the worldly spirit of Renaissance, could well express a new devoutness foreshadowing the coming of the Counter Reformation.

Giovanni Pierluigi, called da Palestrina from the place of his birth, was born about 1525, spent his apprenticeship in the choir of the Roman basilica Santa Maria Maggiore, and then returned to his native town for seven years as choirmaster and organist. Soon after the titular Bishop of Palestrina, Cardinal Giulio del Monte, had been elected pope, assuming the name of Julius III, the choirmaster was made *magister puerorum* of the Capella Julia at St. Peter's. As a token of gratitude, in 1554 Palestrina dedicated the first printed edition of his works, a volume of Masses, to the pope. This volume was followed a year later by his first collection of madrigals. His august patron made him thereafter a member of the Sistine Chapel choir, although as a married man he was not eligible to this quasi-ecclesiastical position. Pope Paul IV, who succeeded Julius III, found this inadmissible, and dismissed Palestrina together with two other married singers. Intrigue, privation, and sickness clouded

his life for years, and although an appointment at St. John's afforded him a precarious existence, Palestrina resigned to return to the church of his childhood, Santa Maria Maggiore. Here he stayed until 1571, when he finally assumed the leadership of the Capella Julia, a position he held until his death in 1594. He was mourned by all Rome and buried with great honor in one of the side chapels of the old Church of St. Peter's. The plate of his coffin bears the inscription "Prince of Music."

With the exception of a few madrigals, Palestrina's whole output was sacred music; and even most of his madrigals were entirely spiritual compositions. Wagner spoke of the "spiritual revelations" engendered by Palestrina's music — "a notion of the essential nature of religion, free from all fictional dogmatic conception."

Actually, Palestrina's art expresses the spirit of the Counter Reformation; he served the new Church current. Meditation, awe, and elation permeate his works; he reflected a new religious consciousness before which the world-conquering, optimistic will of the Renaissance was compelled to retire.

Palestrina hands Pope Marcellus his new Mass. This Mass is regarded as the model of a style of church music which combined an evocative mood with a clear interpretation of the text.

22

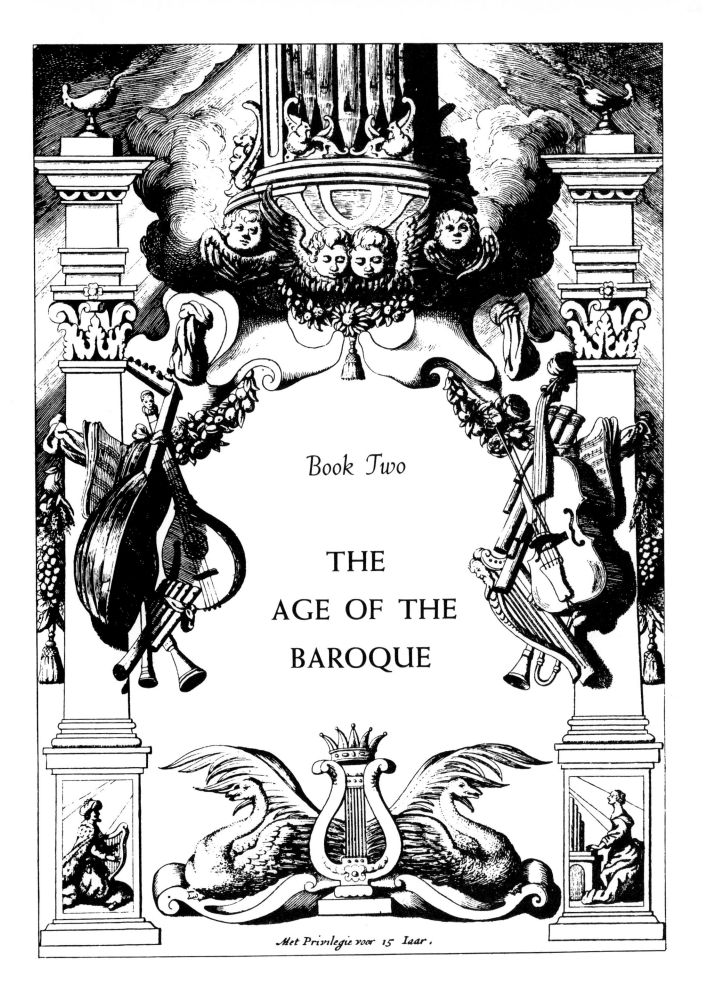

Book Two

THE

AGE OF THE

BAROQUE

Met Privilegie voor 15 Iaar.

A chorus of the Baroque period, inspired by the new plan of a resurgent Church, intones in praise of God. Using more than one orchestra, Giovanni Gabrieli, a Venetian, created a new style of great emotional power and sensuous glow.

Pathos and contemplation were fused in the art of Rubens, Rembrandt, Schütz, and Buxtehude. Rubens: St. Cecilia.

Baroque architecture, like Baroque music, strives for the dramatic, the expressive. Every column suffers, every pillar seems to groan under unbearable pressure. Bernini Altar, St. Peter's, Rome.

Baroque religious sculptors were clearly aware of the warm breath of mysticism and ecstasy — the eroticism of martyrdom. Bernini: St. Theresa.

Baroque Style: Grandiose and Resplendent

As THE RENAISSANCE faded in Europe, Italy, more than any other country, reflected the change of times. The ideals of the Renaissance were safeguarded for some decades, but its soul was stifled, enveloped in the sweep of the Counter Reformation. Schooling and polish, the rich legacy of form and splendor, remained — but the substance had vanished.

Music of warm sonority lifted the faithful into the world of the triumphant Church. Lastmann: Altar scene.

The faithful were lifted from an attitude of quiet devotion, into the world of the triumphant Church. Its cult was celebrated by richly decked clergy under the vaults of a mighty architecture, surrounded by statues and pictures, before scintillating altars ornamented with gold and silver, to the accompaniment of the impressive and resonant music of multiple choirs, orchestras, and organs. All the flame and ardor of the contemporary religious struggles, which often, indeed, involved wild fanaticism, are mirrored in the passionate nature of Baroque art.

The man of the Baroque, animated by a new cerebral fervor, loved unrest and tension and the overwhelmingly pathetic. The Baroque artist frowned upon strict form and harmony of proportions as being too narrow and coercive. The *new* attracted him; and the more astounding, the more contrary to accepted canons of art, the more he welcomed it.

This Baroque search for new effects and dynamic expressiveness appears in the works of the most radical member of the so-called chromatic school, Don Carlo Gesualdo, Prince of Venosa (*ca.*1560–1614). Gesualdo appears as an innovator deeply intrigued by experiments; like some 19th century composers, he seems to have tried his chords and modulations on the keyboard of his instrument, thus arriving at the most sublime, and, at times, the most bizarre, sounds.

Giovanni Gabrieli (1557–1612) was another Baroque composer intent on expanding the frontiers of music. The dramatic and monumental world of the early Baroque is reflected in the vast tonal murals of this Venetian's multiple choirs and in the multitude of instruments that made up his orchestra. The élan and color, the emotional power and sensuous glow of his music overshadowed the great influence and prestige of Palestrinian art. By applying the technique of polychoral writing to instrumental ensembles, Gabrieli laid the foundation of the modern orchestra.

The Birth of Opera

THE SPIRIT of the Counter Reformation — both its strong desire for spiritual regeneration and its penchant for propaganda — found a suitable and sympathetic medium in the Baroque theater. The stage became perhaps the most typical embodiment of the period. The theatrical dominated every form of expression of Baroque art, and even social life assumed a stagelike character.

Historically, classical tragedy originated in the liturgy of Dionysus; it sprang, as has every theater, from a divine cult. When the 16th-century humanists resuscitated the ancient authors, quite naturally they became interested in the theater of antiquity. They staged school dramas whose choruses seemed to evoke the serene atmosphere of the Greek tragedy, heavily charged with religious overtones.

The musical element prominent in the ancient theater also asserted itself once more with the emergence of players and singers. Singing songs to the accompaniment of an instrument was, of course, not new; it had been a fairly common practice ever since the time of the troubadours and Minnesinger. The Baroque, however, developed a new monodic recitative style for individual singers which was capable of conveying both the most delicate shades of human feeling and passion and the complete meaning of the text. Poets and musicians collaborated on this expressive style and built it into a unified musical poetical form — the opera.

Dafne, a tragedy written by Ottavio Rinuccini, a Florentine court poet, and set to music by Jacopo Peri and Giulio Caccini, is generally considered the first opera. However, its music has been lost, so the first really complete opera known to us is *Euridice*. Written by Rinuccini for the marriage of Henry IV of France to Maria de' Medici, with a musical setting supplied by Peri and Caccini, *Euridice* was first performed in the Palazzo Pitti on October 16, 1600.

The design for a musical pageant staged at the marriage of Ferdinand de' Medici and Princess Christine of Lorraine, 1589.

Italian popular comedy involving buffoonery and persiflage relied heavily on musical underscoring. It too helped to pave way for opera.

Many court pageants used chamber orchestras discreetly camouflaged. The size of the chamber orchestra increased during the 17th century until it eventually had to be accommodated in a special orchestra pit.

26

Title page of the score of the first really complete opera, Euridice, published in 1600/1601. The text was by Rinuccini, the score by Caccini and Peri.

A page from the score of Euridice (1600), showing the prologue.

Jacopo Peri playing the role of Arion. As a composer of opera, it was his avowed aim to render musically all shades of his characters' feelings.

The Pythian dragon designed by Bernardo Buontalenti for an early Florentine opera performance.

CLAUDIO MONTEVERDI

Claudio Monteverdi, the outstanding composer of the early Baroque. He created a new dramatic language and greatly expanded the impact of opera.

THE ENORMOUS SUCCESS of *Euridice* assured the future of the new musical dramatic genre, the opera. However, opera still awaited a genius who could raise it above the level of topical and rhetorical festival plays into higher realms of music, a man who would be able to elevate melody and song to their rightful place, not as servants of the drama, but as its very soul. This genius appeared in the person of an extraordinary musician who threw overboard everything that had been forced upon music by learned dilettantes, and created and organized a new form of art.

Claudio Monteverdi (1567–1643) was not only an exceptional musician; he was great because of his powers of meditation and poetical concentration, and the seriousness and perseverance with which he pursued his ideals. He was a creative musical genius whose aim was not to realize the ideals of a distant past, but to express all the life and ardor that was in him. In his *Orfeo*, which we may rightfully consider the first true opera in the history of music, he found a style of such individuality as perhaps no other composer has ever achieved in a first major work. The orchestra was part of the action, reinforcing the psychological expressiveness of the vocal music. It ceased to serve as only a noncommittal background, and instead helped to establish the mood that prevailed on the stage. *Orfeo* contained fourteen independent orchestral pieces or "symphonies." Monteverdi later also developed arias whose melodies were boldly arched, expressive, sculptured.

Monteverdi spent eleven years at the court of the Duke Vincenzo of Mantua. After the Duke's death in 1612, he became choirmaster at St. Mark's in Venice. When he came to Venice, opera had not yet been introduced there, and Monteverdi dedicated himself to the composition of church music, an occupation which was his, ex-officio.

The great epidemic that raged in 1630 dampened the formerly universal enthusiasm for arts and amusements in the Adriatic republic, and the aging master himself turned away from worldly pleasures. He was ordained a priest of the Church in 1630, and retired from the public eye.

Then, the opening of the first public opera house in 1637 and the subsequent enthusiasm of the public for opera electrified Monteverdi and aroused his dramatic genius. He wrote his last great operas, which, judging from the two that were preserved, *Il Ritorno d' Ulisse (The Return of Ulysses)* and *L'Incoronazione di Poppea (The Coronation of Poppea)*, must have been miracles of artistic and dramatic portrayal of the most profound and moving human problems.

THE NEAPOLITAN SCHOOL

Alessandro Scarlatti, *leader of the Neapolitan school of opera.*

As the age of the Baroque moved on, the theater, especially the musical stage, became a passion with all the characteristics of a general madness. There were sixty private theaters in Bologna, not counting those in the convents and colleges. In 1678 one hundred and thirty comedies were performed in private houses in Rome. By the end of the 17th century, over three hundred and fifty different operas had been performed in the sixteen theaters of Venice. The fact that the city had a population of less than 150,000 offers a standard against which we can judge the extent of this operatic craze.

Opera achieved new power as an art form in the hands of the Neapolitan school and its leading spirit, Alessandro Scarlatti. Scarlatti's influence was felt all over Italy, and radiated to France, Germany, and England as well. Every year saw at least one new opera by Scarlatti produced in Rome or in Naples, or in some other Italian city. He created a form of dramatic composition which came to serve all other composers as a model. In Scarlatti's hands the musical forms became more ample, the accompanied recitative acquired a wider field of action, the da capo aria became the most important single element in the dramatic fabric, and the simple curtain raiser developed into the Italian operatic overture.

A stage design for Marc' Antonio Cesti's opera Il Pomo d'Oro. *Francesco Cavalli and Cesti were the leaders of Venetian opera, carrying on the tradition of Monteverdi.*

Opera in France: Lully

IN FRANCE the fusion of music and drama into opera occurred quite naturally because of the tradition of the French ballet.

Ballets had always been an indispensable part of Renaissance pageantry; indeed, the so-called "court ballet," despite its simple title, was the French bid for the reconstruction of classical tragedy, for besides spoken parts and dances, these festive displays utilized recitatives, and songs.

The many eminent Italians at the French 17th Century court, headed by the queen, Marie de' Medici, undoubtedly promoted interest in the dramatized ballet. The musical component of these presentations received new impetus when shortly after he assumed political power, Cardinal Mazarin invited a little group of Roman singers to give opera performances in Paris. The cardinal, anxious to acquaint France with the form of entertainment most admired in his native country, sponsored some elaborate operatic stagings, among them Luigi Rossi's *Orfeo*, performed on March 2, 1647. These stagings had an enthusiastic reception by the public at large.

Twenty years passed before opera began to show evidence that its roots had taken hold in French soil, by which time its most powerful, if not very lovable, pro-

ponent was Jean Baptiste Lully (1632–1687). Florentine by birth, French by education, Lully brought French opera to the height of a great art. At the beginning of his career he was not interested in opera, but wrote ballets, took part in performances as an actor, conducted the orchestra, and, most of all, kept a close watch on the events at court. In 1661 he succeeded in

Jean Baptiste Lully, a great organizer and musical genius. He was the true creator of French opera.

30

winning the appointment of "superintendent" of the king's music. Eliminating his political adversaries by fair means and foul, he became in 1672 absolute master of the situation.

This sinister schemer, brilliant businessman, and real estate dealer who amassed a fortune of millions of francs, this inveterate Don Juan, was a musician and artist endowed with supreme gifts. Lully's works were not called operas, but lyrical tragedies. He achieved the creation and development of the form and language of the lyric tragedy, the French opera. He could not have done this if he did not possess a truly dramatic temperament and rich imagination, part of his Italian heritage; but the melodic line of his vocal parts reflects the inner laws of the French language.

Lully's reputation and glory were immense. Italian, German, and English musicians came to study with him, and his music, the confluence of many musical rivers, was widely imitated throughout Europe.

Opera in England: Purcell

IF FRANCE HAD its ballet, England excelled in its "masques," a genre which was the British adaptation of the Italian popular theater and the French ballet. Masques quickly established themselves in England; but it appears that music was secondary to drama in these courtly presentations.

The operatic medium flowered in England in the works by Henry Purcell, who — like Lully in France — became the model for all English composers. Though Purcell was a church composer by vocation and by profession, his dramatic gifts drove him toward the stage, and toward the arbiter of contemporaneous drama, Dryden. The result of their collaboration, *King Arthur* (1691), was not really an opera, but rather a play with music. Other dramatic works in the same style were *Dioclesian* (1690), *The Indian Queen* (1695), *The Faërie Queene* (1692), and the Shakespearean "arrangements," *Timon of Athens* (1694) and *The Tempest* (1695). It must be admitted, however, that no matter how beautiful most of this music is, it remains incidental music in which ornamentation takes the place of dramatic expression and characterization through music. Only one true opera from Purcell's pen is known to us — *Dido and*

A genius was lost when Henry Purcell died at 36, at the height of his powers.

Aeneas — a work whose music dramatizes the action and brings to life the emotional atmosphere of this famous love story.

It has often been pointed out that Purcell's music abounds in foreign elements. Nonetheless, his unbridled imagination, his free and original forms, transmuted every inspiration, however French or Italian in appearance, into his own creation.

Ascendancy of the Violin

T HE BAROQUE OPERA was the art form which united in itself all that this virtuoso era had produced. It was an art which glorified in melodious beauty, and exploited the human voice to the ultimate. The operatic melody knew no law of aesthetics other than its own bewitching and intoxicating sensuous beauty, and the coloraturas of the virtuoso singers dominated the entire apparatus.

With this kind of virtuosity as their model, it was quite natural that the Italian composers would direct their attention to the violin, the most sensitively expressive of instruments and the one most closely akin to the human voice. By the beginning of the second decade of the 17th century, the violin had become the favorite orchestral and solo instrument, outdistancing the softer and less imperious gamba. The composer who came to embody the ideals of classical Italian violin music, and the man who united all the threads developed by his eminent colleagues, was Arcangelo Corelli (1653–1713). His writing for the violin invoked the sensuous expressiveness of the human voice; his melodies soar boldly and are filled with noble pathos and a serious and sublime lyricism; he maintained a just balance between instrumental sonority and polyphonic construction.

At the same time Corelli perfected one of the most fascinating products of Baroque orchestral music, the concerto grosso. The first instrumental concertos, which opposed, in an application of the echo principle, a small body of instruments and a large one, appeared in the last quarter of the 17th century. Corelli gave the concerto grosso its definitive form — a *concertino* of two violins and a cello or gamba which played in alternating sections with the *concerto*, also called the *ripieno* — that is, the whole orchestra. Corelli's twelve Concerti Grossi (Opus 6), were published in 1712, and evince a rich sonority, and variety of form and expression.

The 18th century built on the foundation established by Corelli. All the great Italian composers of the magnificent violin

The concertmaster of the Sun King's orchestra doubled as conductor.

The lute, queen of Renaissance instruments, declined when the sonorous harpsichord became the favorite instrument.

The viola da gamba, more subdued than the violin, became less important in the orchestra, but remained in favor as a chamber music instrument.

school were, indeed, either pupils of the master, or continued his art. Among the great violinists of this era were Tommaso Vitali (c.1665–c.1740), Antonio Vivaldi (c. 1678–1743), Francesco Geminiani (1687–1762), and Pietro Locatelli (1693–1764), the last two pupils of Corelli. These men were perhaps the most eminent among a host of great artists. They were all superb musicians, thoroughly versed in the art of composition; and if they abandoned Corelli's architectonic poise, it was not because they lacked technique or inspiration. They were great performers, in love with their instrument, which itself was a work of art with a soul beneath its wood and strings.

Antonio Vivaldi (left) *enlarged the solo passages in the concerto grosso until the solo violin dominated. Arcangelo Corelli* (center), *co-creator of the most fascinating Baroque instrumental form, the concerto grosso. Francesco Veracini* (right) *was considered by some as a great violinist, by others an eccentric.*

The Violin Family

Every art depends on its means of expression; and it is no accident that the great Italian school of violin composition flourished at the time when Stradivari, the famous Cremona instrument maker, had finished his apprenticeship and found his own style. After the "long Stradivarius" appeared about 1690, the violin became progressively broader and more arched, until, in the first decade of the 18th century, it reached that unsurpassable symmetry which made the name of Stradivari synonymous with purity of tone and craftsmanship.

The Hellier Stradivarius, dated 1679.

Stradivari in his workshop.

Antonius Stradiuarius Cremonensis
Faciebat Anno 1719

Stradivari's trademark.

Claudio Merulo (1533–1604), first of the great organ virtuosi. His performances excited boundless admiration.

Baroque Organ and the Fugal Style

DURING THE BAROQUE, the violin assumed a star role in the orchestra. Yet the strings were limited in range and body. The organ, with its dynamic range and great variety of color combinations, was the Baroque instrument par excellence — and in spite of the seemingly archaic nature of the chief forms of organ literature. Of these, fugue and chorale variation were deeply rooted in the old traditions of polyphony; but organ toccatas and fantasies, with their rhapsodic atmosphere, rippling passagework, bold modulations, and fascinating ornamental superstructure, were Baroque to the core.

The outstanding master of the early Baroque keyboard style was Girolamo Frescobaldi (1583–1644), organist at St. Peter's in Rome. This inspired musician, famed all over the world for his virtuosity and rare ability to improvise, opened a new epoch in the history of instrumental music by using the keyboard in an extraordinarily personal expressive style. His creative imagination enriched the forms of instrumental music — toccata, ricercar, canzone, fantasy, fugue — with a passionate, almost feverish, poetry and an austere pathos.

Jan Pieterszoon Sweelinck (1562–1621), a Dutch organist and composer, taught so many German musicians that he was called "the maker of German organists."

Girolamo Frescobaldi (1583–1644) excelled in the composition of toccatas, a name derived from the Italian tocarre, *to touch the keys. The toccata eventually became a monumental virtuoso piece.*

Medieval organs required a strong operator. To sound a tone, the player pulled out a slide at the base of a pipe, thus allowing the air to rush in.

Organ wagon designed by Dürer for the triumphal pageant of Emperor Maximilian.

Cut-away view of the mechanism of a 17th-18th-century organ. Its physical and tonal expansion was made possible by the advances made in acoustics during the 17th century.

The collegia musica, *secular musical societies, were an evidence of the Germans' love for intimate music making and their preference for instrumental forms.*

The Protestant Baroque: Cantatas and Oratorios

IN ITALY AND FRANCE, opera was in the foreground of musical life. But the rank and file of Germans, deeply distressed by the Thirty Years' war and its aftermath, turned to religious music. The specific character of Protestant Christianity shaped this music, and the congregation formed its point of departure. Congregation-consciousness speaks with convincing force in the Protestant chorales, which form the basis of this whole art, and in the cantatas and oratorios which are the greatest treasures of Protestant church art. These are more than mere art forms; they are an elemental interpretation of the words of the Bible, the essence of Protestant thought.

For the Protestant people of the central and northern German states, the church was an asylum, a symbol of protection; within it they found solace. The solemn music they heard there gave them their much-desired illusion of the peaceful existence in the hereafter. The smaller churches were often served entirely by amateur musicians recruited from the ranks of the citizens. They participated in the services not only from their love of music but because, being faithful Lutherans, they were convinced that church music served the glory of God and the benefit of the congregation.

This deeply religious nature of the German Baroque found an outlet in the cantata and oratorio. Oratorios may be described as spiritual operas, dealing with religious themes. The components of the German oratorio were many: the concerto, the chorale, the opera recitative. Textually its greatest inspiration was drawn from the story of the Passion of the Lord, from the Last Supper to the last words of the Re-

Title page of Little Spiritual Concertos *for four voices and organ by Heinricus Sagittarius — a Latinized version of Heinrich Schütz.*

36

deemer. Heinrich Schütz was the first composer to fuse all these elements.

Heinrich Schütz (1585–1672) studied in Venice with the renowned master Giovanni Gabrieli. The young German musician had arrived in 1609 in what then was the capital of the musical world, where germinated the epoch-making changes which were to conquer the music of all Europe. Schütz was deeply impressed by the tonal and technical discoveries of the Venetians, and stayed among them until the death of Gabrieli in 1612. When he returned to Germany he translated the Venetian ideas — monody, polychoral writing, and the concerto — into his native idiom. The spell of Italian music is evident in his work; but the spiritual roots of his art are deeply set in German soil.

Like Monteverdi, Haydn, and Verdi, Schütz composed his greatest works at an age when other people finish their earthly careers. The aged master, who had declared himself passionately for the brilliant, expressive, and modern music which emanated from Italy, eventually returned to the great traditions of his Germanic forebears. *The History of the Suffering and Death of Our Lord and Saviour Jesus Christ* (1665–66), four settings of the Passion using the texts of the four Gospels, renounces all the external advantages of the Italian style. No instruments are employed, even the recitatives being set in the old unaccompanied manner.

Heinrich Schütz at 88. His music, inspired by Italian forms, expressed the depths of German Protestant religious feeling.

Schütz among his singers in the Schlosskirche *of Dresden. His church concertos were precursors of the German cantatas.*

Athanasius Kircher (1602–1680), a learned Jesuit priest of the 17th century, who wrote a treatise on music.

Robert Fludd's Temple of Music related harmony to architectural proportions.

Music: Art or Science

BAROQUE OPERA and oratorio excelled in the expression of human emotions. But the age of Baroque emotionalism is also the age of the great rationalists: Kepler, Descartes, and Locke. This duality of reason and emotion is reflected in the music of the 17th century; the temper of the period prompted some composers, usually of considerable learning and education to defend their technique of composition by scientific dissertations. They felt that however inspired their art was, it would gain status if it could be explained and analysed on a rational basis. Music struggled for equality with science — for to be classified as a science was to be accorded a higher intellectual rank.

Conversely scientists became interested in the phenomena of music. Gottfried Wilhelm Leibniz (1646–1716), one of the greatest mathematicians of the period, called music "the unconscious arithmetic of the soul." Kepler wrote extensively on the harmony of the heavens. He held that the planets, because of their varying degrees of velocity, produce different sounds which combine into a celestial symphony. Other scholars tried to establish a structure of laws governing harmony. Athanasius Kircher (1602–1680), a celebrated German polyhistorian and one of the most learned men of the century, attempted to give a psychological explanation for the existence of different styles of music.

38

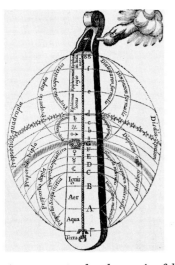

A universe in the shape of a fiddle designed by Robert Fludd. He revived the Pythagorean theory of the harmony of the spheres, which held that man's soul must be attuned to the laws of the universe.

A music museum was established in Rome by Michel Todini, an experimenter in acoustics and builder of musical machines. The player shown here, perhaps Todini himself, is controlling through one keyboard (A) the three other instruments (B, C, D) in the background.

Kircher's broadcasting system. In this typically 17th-century mixture of science and fancy, conversations from the courtyard (at left) are transmitted through a sound channel (G). Or, a supervisor can convey messages to the courtyard by talking through the "microphone" (E).

39

Johann Sebastian Bach. Detail from Bach monument at Leipzig.

Johann Sebastian Bach

Toward the end of the 17th century, clear lines of demarcation emerged between the two great cultural territories of Germany. The German south, with its two musical centers in Vienna and Munich, was dominated by ecstatic church music, brilliant opera, and scintillating Italian violin music. Music in the German north was less brilliant, more intimate, and more serious. Although northern composers accepted many innovations from the south, their works had a more popular character. Protestant Germany never accorded Italian opera the prominence it attained in Italy and France, except in Hamburg, as opera remained a courtly entertainment largely unknown to the citizenry, which sought its musical pleasures in the church, the musical societies, and the home.

These fundamental German traits notwithstanding, it was inevitable that opera, slowly reaching every part of Germany, would leave its mark on German Protestant music. Musicians acquainted with the opera and cantata of the Italians became weary of the "monotonous congregational singing" and attempted to exploit the elements of Italian dramatic composition — aria, duet, recitative — which had first appeared in German music with Schütz, and a process of rapprochement began between church music and opera.

The final fusion of the two was accomplished in the Cantatas and Passions of Johann Sebastian Bach (1685–1750), whose work represents the final synthesis of all that the Baroque gave to music.

Although Bach used elements derived from contemporary opera, his music was not a true expression of his times; he belonged to the old Lutheran world of the preceding generation, a stranger amid the rising secular music of the 18th century. His art rests on the traditions of the German Reformation, which achieved its highest manifestation in him, in the midst of the era of the Enlightenment. His mysterious and singularly Gothic nature is reflected in compositions expressing a faith that was on the wane, a faith that lived in the writing of Luther and the paintings of Dürer. In Bach's work speaks a man who, rising above earthly confusion, was entirely immersed in the worship of the celestial.

Choral group and instrumentalists performing during an 18th-century church service.

Hans Bach, town fiddler, an early member of the Bach clan which provided music at dances and other civic occasions. In some German towns "a Bach" automatically meant "a musician."

BACH'S PILGRIMAGES

DYNASTIES ARE NOT uncommon in the history of music, but the Bach family's is unrivaled and unparalleled. Over fifty of its members were actively engaged in the musical profession, and a number of them were among the great masters of their art. One branch of the clan provided the city of Erfurt with so many good organists and town musicians that they were called "the Bachs" even when there was no longer a bearer of the family name among them.

Johann Sebastian was born in 1685, the son of Ambrosius Bach, a town musician in Eisenach. Having lost his parents at an early age, the boy's education was entrusted to an older brother, Johann Christoph (1671–1721), a pupil of the famous organist, Pachelbel. In 1700 a scholarship enabled young Bach to enter St. Michael's School in Lüneburg, where he came into contact with serious musical culture.

In 1703 the eighteen-year-old Bach was appointed court violinist in the ducal orchestra at Weimar, and in the same year he received the more comfortable position of organist of the new church in Arnstadt. Master of a fine new organ, with duties not at all taxing and with a good salary, he was ideally placed for creative activity. After a couple of years' service, he took a leave of absence to go on a pilgrimage to Lübeck to hear Dietrich Buxtehude (1637–1707), the greatest organ master of the period.

Buxtehude's fugues, his virtuoso preludes with their racing and rumbling pedal passages, and his capricious themes fascinated Bach, and left indelible marks on his own style.

Restless ever since his visit to Lübeck, in 1707 Bach accepted an invitation to become organist at St. Blasius', in Mühlhausen. But within less than a year he moved to Weimar as court organist to Duke Wilhelm Ernst. The compositions of this period reflect his many duties at the ducal court; and the majority of his organ works were composed in the nine years he spent at Weimar.

During the time he was composing for the ducal orchestra and developing his instrumental style, Bach was admired mainly as an organ player, and was repeatedly invited to examine and play newly-installed organs. His fame seemed to mean little at the court, however, and, dissatisfied, Bach left in 1717 to become court conductor to the Prince of Anhalt-Cöthen.

As conductor of an eighteen-piece orchestra charged with furnishing chamber music for court festivities, Bach produced during this period much chamber music and many concertos, including *The Brandenburg Concertos*. Here he also finished the first part of the *Well-Tempered Clavier*. His days at Cöthen were among the happiest of Bach's life; yet they ended in tragedy, for his young wife died in 1720.

Bach in his early thirties. He was probably in Weimar when this portrait was done.

Church of Arnstadt where Bach started his career as organist and cantor.

Duke Wilhelm Ernst made Bach concertmaster of a twenty-piece orchestra, but awarded the conductorship to another musician.

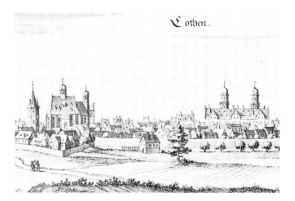

The Court of Anhalt-Cöthen offered Bach a conductorship in 1717. During his six years at Cöthen Bach produced some of his greatest chamber and harpsichord music.

View of Leipzig, with St. Thomas' Church in the background. Mercury leaning over the clavier (left) symbolizes Leipzig's role as a center of music and trade.

After Bach had married a second wife, Anna Magdalena, he cast about for a new home near good Lutheran schools. Johann Kuhnau, the cantor of the Thomasschule in Leipzig, had died in 1722, and his desirable position was vacant. But the application of the famous organist Bach was not very favorably received, because the municipal council wanted to hire a man who was musically less conservative than Bach was considered to be. The council only consented to hiring him after both Telemann and Graupner, who were identified with the modern Italian style, were found to be unavailable. It was not without misgivings that Bach exchanged the position of a court conductor for that of a municipal music director; and his fears were justified by his ensuing quarrels with the rector of the school, the consistory, the university, and the municipality. Despite the strife, the Leipzig period was nevertheless rich in titanic creations: The Passions, the Masses, *The Christmas Oratorio*, a great number of monumental cantatas and organ works, as well as the fugues of the second volume of the *Well-Tempered Clavier*, and other contrapuntal epics. During the last decade of his life, the master found enjoyment in the musical abilities of his sons and in a few journeys which carried him to Dresden and to Potsdam to a memorable meeting with Frederick the Great.

The constant copying of music had ruined his eyesight, which failed him altogether in the last year of his life. He died in 1750, and was buried in the churchyard of St. John's. His grave was lost among the nameless, and became the object of scientific search on the two-hundredth anniversary of his birth. Learned anatomists and anthropologists identified one of the exhumed bodies as his, and he was laid to rest in a sarcophagus in the same church.

A cantata performance of the period of
Bach, showing details of the orchestra. This
engraving was published in 1732 in J. G.
Walther's musical dictionary.

St. Thomas' Church (right) as it appeared in
1723, the year Bach assumed his cantorate.
Here he wrote hundreds of cantatas.

For the choir of St. Thomas' Church and
young singers, like those shown here, Bach
created six magnificent motets, among them
Sing Ye to the Lord for eight voices.

BACH'S CHORAL WORKS

THE CENTER of Lutheran religion is the
inner struggle of the individual. This
traditional subjective religion was accepted
with the deepest conviction by the Bach
family. Its ardor, humility, fear, and soaring
hope are embodied in Bach's cantatas with
an intensity and effect which make these
works the highest expression of Lutheran
religiousness.

The variety of his cantatas is great,
although certain types can be discerned
among them. There are religious pastorals,
oratorio-like dramatic scenes, Biblical episodes, and transfigurations which are steeped
in pious contemplation and filled with mystic symbolism.

All the stock devices of the Baroque
era parade before us in Bach's cantatas: the

introductory sonata or sinfonia, the da capo aria, the operatic arioso and recitative, the French overture (occasionally transformed into choruses), the concerto, the scintillating trumpet fanfares, the multiple choirs of the early Baroque.

Still, unlike his colleagues and predecessors, Bach could never free himself from the chorale or the Scriptures. This created a somewhat anachronistic situation, for by the time that the master was finally resolving a relationship between old and new, between the chorale and the opera, the chorale had already ceased to be a living force.

Bach's cantatas determined his choral style not only by their sheer bulk, but because they carried him through the whole gamut of musical expression. All the choral works follow the cantata style faithfully, the only difference being one of proportions. Thus the so-called *Christmas Oratorio* is simply a string of cantatas, while the Passions carry the cantata, and with it Protestant church music, to its ultimate height.

While seemingly an entirely different work, the *B minor Mass* is also a collection of monumental cantatas. Gigantic concerted motets in the old five-part setting alternate with suave and mellow duets; arias are relieved by colossal double choirs and followed by coloratura arias with an obbligato instrument in the Venetian-Neapolitan manner.

The *St. John Passion,* the earlier of the two oratorios extant of the four composed by Bach, is more youthful and impetuous than the later *St. Matthew Passion.* The *St. John Passion* presents the liturgical drama in a summary, vehement, manner. Its dramatic quality is especially evident in the recitatives, brusquely interrupted by the chorus of the people.

Christian Henrici (1700–1764), the librettist of the *Passion according to St. Matthew,* was not a poet of particular distinction, but in his arrangement Bach found the elements he needed: on the one hand the solid churchly tradition, the unaltered narration of the Evangelist, dramatized by the choral settings of the cries of the people and the oratory of the soloists; on the other, the tender reflections upon the Lord's sufferings which correspond to the feelings of the guilty and thankful soul, longing for redemption.

With the *St. Matthew Passion* we arrive at the end of the history of the musical setting of the Biblical drama. Bach's works carried the genre to its ultimate and unsurpassable height. The oratorio continued to flourish, and the succeeding generations produced many masterpieces in this form; but the elemental Lutheran faith and strength of conviction which produced the Passions of Bach vanished, together with the appreciation of the works which so nobly expressed it in music.

Entrance to St. Thomas' Church and view of its interior during a Sunday service.

BACH'S INSTRUMENTAL WORKS

As a vocal composer Bach shows indisputable limitations in spite of his almost oppressive greatness; in his instrumental music he stands before us unrivaled and above any criticism, aesthetic or technical. In spite of the overwhelming bulk of his vocal works, Bach's real and most personal domain is instrumental music, especially organ music. The spirit of the organ is expressed everywhere in the cantata-symphonies, and in the wondrous polyphonic sonatas for unaccompanied violin; and many of his clavier compositions, especially some of the preludes and fugues of the *Well-Tempered Clavier*, are much closer to organ technique than to any kind of clavichord or harpsichord playing.

In the lyric poems called chorale preludes Bach the organist expressed his most personal and profound beliefs. The chorale preludes range in size from illuminated miniatures of a dozen measures to large murals of chorale fantasies and fugues. Bach carried these poetic compositions to a spiritual and artistic depth which could not be fathomed by his contemporaries. Even as a young man he was reprimanded by the consistory of Arnstadt for his manner of playing the chorales: "We charge him with having hitherto been in the habit of making surprising *variationes* in the chorales, and intermixing divers strange sounds, so that thereby the congregation were confounded."

Bach's most personal domain was organ music. His proud preludes and fugues, with their splendor and sentiment, made the organ the "queen of instruments."

First prelude of the Well-Tempered Clavier, a collection dedicated by Bach "to the musical youth zealous to learn." In this work he showed that all twenty-four minor and major scales, many of them previously neglected, could be used to expand the tonal scope of keyboard music.

Johann Kuhnau, Bach's predecessor at Leipzig, adapted the Italian chamber sonata to the keyboard. Bach's own Clavierübung (1726–1733) explored this new style.

Bach's clavier music stems from many ancestors, its lineage going back to Sweelinck. But the most lasting influence was derived from the works of J. C. F. Fischer and Johann Kuhnau.

Bach's preludes, inventions, suites and partitas for harpsichord are all genre pieces of endless charm, full of moving content. The *French Suites, English Suites* (which are also in the French manner), and the

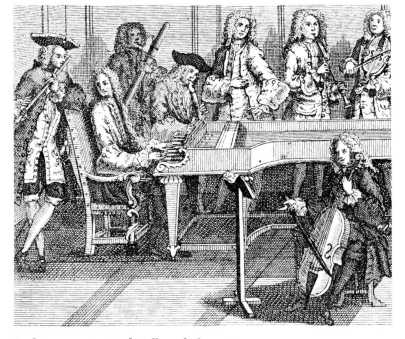

In his concertos Bach followed the pattern set by Vivaldi with its counterplay of solo instrument and orchestra.

dance pieces which are to be found in the various *Clavierbüchlein* written for his sons and his wife, show Bach's complete mastery of the French style of Couperin. Over the feathery touch of his dance suites, however, the agreeably pointed rhythm, and the sweet melancholy, the German master pours the poetic warmth of a lyricist inspired to meditation where his French colleagues are merely seeking entertainment.

Bach composed the *Well-Tempered Clavier* to exploit the possibilities inherent in the major-minor scales with twelve identical intervals which had been developed by Andreas Werckmeister.

The fugues of the second volume, in particular, showed an astonishing growth of the composer's polyphonic imagination, which reached its culmination in the *Art of Fugue.*

Next to the fugue, the Italian concerto or concerto grosso as developed by Corelli and Vivaldi seems to have been the form which most interested Bach from the time of his first contact with Italian music. The *Brandenburg Concertos*, the concerto for two violins, and those for two and more pianos all belong to this genre. Bach's *Brandenburg Concertos* open with that busy and animated tone which characterizes commissioned social music, ordered for and performed at official functions, academic convocations, or banquets. It behooved this type of concerto to be spirited, clever, and well-built. But the social spirit of program music vanishes in the middle movements before a profundity of feeling. The Bach of these middle movements is no longer the consummate instrumental virtuoso; these adagios are Passion music, and belong to the greatest poetic achievements of the German spirit.

In his chamber music for a restricted number of instruments, Bach did not experiment with anything new; instead he carried the traditional and established to its ultimate destination. In so doing he often reached the limits of musical reality and human ingenuity. Nowhere is this more evident than in the sonatas and suites written for an unaccompanied violin. Fantastic preludes, completely developed fugues, and cyclopean variations alternate with graceful dances in these sonatas. Creative imagination reaches in them its absolute triumph.

Leonardo Vinci, a Neapolitan composer.

Antonio Montanari, a virtuoso violinist.

Instrumentalists in the Age of Bach and Handel

DURING THE Baroque period Italy's bustling musical life found a chronicler of candor and wit in the artist Pier Leone Ghezzi (1674–1755). Some of his sketches are here reproduced for the first time.

Ghezzi was born in Rome and seems to have spent most of his life in the Eternal City. Whenever a singer or an instrumental virtuoso arrived in Rome, Ghezzi seems to

have been on hand to chronicle the event with the promptness of a modern news photographer. Besides drawing the musicians, he attached lengthy captions which give us much valuable information. A typical report: "Faustina, a famous Venetian singer . . . passed through Rome, stayed at the Palace of the Colonna, and sang there many hours . . . before leaving for Venice,

Don August, a parish priest, played the violin and viola d'amore with great sweetness.

Father Don Philipp, a Bernardine monk, and an accomplished cembalist.

Gennaro Amelia from Naples, a cellist, who came to Rome in 1744.

Fabbio Orsini from Naples, a good player of the great lute.

(Viewed by an Artist-Chronicler)

March 20, 1722. I saw her at the Colonna's and made this memento. This woman is well educated and not at all difficult."

Aside from famous performers, Ghezzi met many of the outstanding composers of his time — especially those attached to the court of Cardinal Ottoboni. This patron of the arts sponsored his own academy, which attracted musicians from all over Italy as well as from other countries. Alessandro Scarlatti appeared at the Ottoboni palace to conduct his cantatas, and Corelli staged his chamber works there. At one soirée in 1709 a young musician from Saxony appeared, *"il caro Sassone,"* Georg Friedrich Händel. Ghezzi has left us vivid pictures of these and other musicians who were famous at the height of the Baroque.

The prompter in his box during an opera performance in the Teatro Della Pace in Rome, 1725.

Peter Sterlichi, a good violoncellist, who left Rome to play in Spain.

A portrait drawing of Handel, done at the height of his career.

George Frideric Handel

BACH SEEMED unaware of the existence of a public and was completely satisfied with his choir loft, the *collegium musicum,* and the concert room of a small princely residence. In contrast, George Frideric Handel was a citizen of the world. He enjoyed life to the full, and at the same time showed an unlimited creative capacity. Ad-

Handel's London. A musician in a Venetian gondola is accompanied by a singer who floats along on a bass fiddle.

Handelian pomp was most adequately displayed in the Royal Fireworks Music, *which was scored for an orchestra unusually large for the period.*

versity and debacle had no meaning for him; the harder he was hit, the more determined was his resurgence. His undertakings were hazardous; he gambled with his forces and threw his reserves into the melee before they were needed. Because of the vast forum in which he appeared, and the large public to which he could address himself — two advantages denied to Bach — his fame and influence were tremendous even in his lifetime. He became an institution in England while Bach was a provincial cantor quibbling with the petty school authorities in Leipzig.

Born in 1685, Händel (later Anglicized as Handel) received the customary education of a German musician. When he arrived in Hamburg in 1703 the world of opera must have been a revelation, after the cantor's music to which he was accustomed. But there is no trace of any hesitation on his part, for the young com-

poser entered into the spirit of the theater with the greatest ease, producing two years later his first opera, *Armida*. Having acquired a certain reputation, although only twenty-one years old, he left the Hanseatic city in 1706 to go to Italy, the promised land of musicians. Here he won his earliest acclaim with his opera *Rodrigo*. This work earned him the favor of the famous singer Vittoria Tesi, for whom he wrote the exacting title role of his second Italian opera, *Agrippina*. Performed in 1709 in Venice, the work achieved such a stormy success that its creator became one of the most noted composers in Italy.

On his return to Germany, the Elector of Hanover invited Handel to become Hanoverian court conductor. In 1712 Handel moved to London; after the House of Hanover assumed the English crown in 1714, Handel remained in London until the end of his life, in 1759.

HANDEL'S OPERAS

In England Handel stepped into a bee-hive of activity. Italian opera was the rage, Italian singers ruled — even the use of English librettos had been abandoned without a murmur. By 1711 the Italian opera had become firmly established in the Haymarket Theater, and in the same year the English managers of the Drury Lane Theater decided to discontinue the production of English musical works.

This operatic frenzy coincided with the speculative spirit of the times which was responsible for the prodigious success of the South Sea Company. The Royal Academy of Music, an operatic undertaking sponsored by the king and patterned after the Académie Royale de Musique, was founded in 1720 in the midst of this atmosphere. One of the directors was Handel, who undertook the assembling of the personnel himself. The season of 1720 started under brilliant auspices, but rivalry and intrigue, and the phenomenal success of *Beggar's Opera*, gradually undermined the institution. The Academy failed in 1728, after having produced a number of Handelian operas that became known all over Europe. Three other attempts to put opera — especially Handelian opera — back on its feet also ended in disaster, despite Handel's phenomenal energy as an entrepreneur and composer.

Carlo Broschi, called Farinelli, in a female role. He was perhaps the most famous castrato. Handel and his London antagonists vied for his services.

Interior of the Court Theatre in Dresden, Saxony, a center of musical activity, situated not far from Halle, Handel's birthplace.

BEGGAR'S OPERA

English popular opposition to Italian operas became increasingly articulate with the success of the most important indigenous product of the English Baroque lyric theater, the ballad opera. *Beggar's Opera* (1728), a clever satire on the conventional Italian opera, remains the most spirited example of this genre. John Gay (1685–1732), a satirist of society and folklore of London's streets, wrote the excellent text; the music was arranged by a Prussian musician, John Christopher Pepusch (1667–1752), who, like Handel, had found a second home in England. *Beggar's Opera* achieved a sensational success. Produced by John Rich in 1728, its phenomenal success made "Gay rich and Rich gay."

The public's joy and very real amusement in listening to an evening of familiar and much-loved music, to a witty and intelligible text in their own tongue, explains the popularity of the ballad operas and their adverse effect on the imported Italian species. Italian opera was defeated, and even the intrepid Handel was obliged to seek another field of action.

William Hogarth, English painter and satirist, expressed popular antagonism toward Italian opera. Pietro Castrucci, violinist of the opera, is shown at the window dismayed at hearing the popular tune The Lady's Fall *from the* Beggar's Opera.

The prison scene from the Beggar's Opera, *a painting by William Hogarth.*

John Heidegger, Handel's librettist and business partner.

ORATORIO: RELIGIOUS DRAMA IN MUSIC

In his oratorios Handel gave England a national substitute for opera. The oratorio was not humble church music, but musical and dramatic entertainment on a high moral plane, close to and befitting English taste. In these magnificent choral works Handel glorified the rise of the free people of England. The people of Israel were presented as prototypes of the English nation, the chosen people of God reincarnated in Christendom; and magnificent psalms of thanksgiving and victory marches of imperial Baroque splendor proclaimed the grandiose awareness of England's world-conquering power.

The public which had spurned Handel's operas turned avidly to his edifying, colorful, and massive oratorios, seeing in their monumental Biblical choruses its own triumphal progress and recognizing in them its own religious feeling.

Handel's first oratorio, *Esther (or Hamman and Mordecai)*, was in reality a masque; *Semele, Alexander Balus,* and *Susanna* are chorus operas; *Deborah, Israel in Egypt, Belshazzar, Judas Maccabaeus* are gigantic choral tragedies. The operatic origins of the oratorios are indicated in their division into three acts; and although the main force of this new dramatic style was the chorus, Handel could not entirely give up arias, duets, and recitatives — they were in his blood.

The most famous Handelian oratorio is *Messiah,* which to the public at large has come to represent the epitome of the oratorio and the height of Handel's art. Handel wrote the music for *Messiah* in twenty-four

days, working as one possessed. From a musical point of view it stands alone in Handel's output because of its lyric and contemplative nature. Immediately after *Messiah* was completed, the master returned to the dramatic oratorio. In *Samson,* the first part of which was completed two weeks after *Messiah,* Handel presented historical people opposing each other in fierce dramatic action, a situation which is perhaps the true essence of the Handelian oratorio.

Handel (at right, standing) with his musicians and singers. This was the kind of group, of about fifty performers, which presented Handel's dramatic oratorios.

The last line of Handel's manuscript of Messiah.

HANDEL'S INSTRUMENTAL WORKS

Handel's instrumental works exhibit a synthesis of the most heterogeneous musical styles. The *Concerti Grossi,* which, with Bach's *Brandenburg Concertos,* crowned all efforts of Baroque orchestral music, conserved a great deal of the noble tone and brilliant virtuosity of the Italian string style — but the gestures are larger, the melodic arches wider, and the form and logic of construction more monumental in their straightforwardness. Once an allegro movement is started, it rolls along with the impetuousness of a mountain stream, while the broad pathos of the slow movements spins garlands around quietly ambling melodies. Handel's chamber music and keyboard music is also many-sided, drawing on a multitude of sources. From the point of view of stylistic and formal development, many of the keyboard pieces are notable because they so clearly indicate how the older type of instrumental suite was changing into the newer, sonatalike construction; others, however, are written in an entirely free form.

Handel the Performer. *Painting by J. Thornhill. Fitzwilliam Museum, Cambridge.*

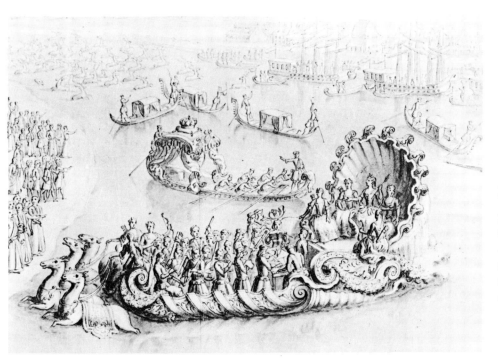

Handel wrote his Water Music *to be played on a trip George I made in 1717 from Lambeth down the Thames, in a barge similar to the one pictured here.*

55

A celebration of the hundredth anniversary of Handel's birthday was held in 1785 in Westminster Abbey. Hundreds of singers and players participated.

The Handel monument by Roubillac in Westminster Abbey.

Book Three

FROM

ROCOCO

TO

CLASSICISM

Rococo society moved in a fanciful, poetic world of pastorals and masquerades, the world painted by Watteau. Watteau's counterpart in music was Couperin. His musical genre pieces depicted in sound the painter's fêtes galantes.

François Couperin, called the Great. Like the Rococo painters, he concentrated on small character pieces in which temperament was controlled, emotions measured.

Early 18th-century garden musicale.

58

Musically the Rococo is most typically expressed in little clavecin pieces burdened with ornamentations and grace notes.

The Rococo: Sophisticated Playfulness

THE 18TH CENTURY was engrossed in dismantling the edifice that the Baroque had built, and that great monument of style began to crumble before the final stones were carried to its summit. The essence of the new artistic creed, and the idea that animated everything from political philosophy to music, was an urge for liberty: liberation from the rules that had become stereotyped, from the stylistic conventions that had become rigid, from the artistic forms that had become immutable. All this represented a violently powerful insurrection against the motive power of the Baroque.

The Baroque sought to crush, to convert, to exalt, and to bring about redemption; the Rococo wished to entertain. The dramatic intensity, the rhetoric and pathos of the Baroque gave way to an intimate, witty, graceful, polished and entertaining art — the *style galant*. The Rococo presented the world with lighthearted, amoral, and beautiful entertainments — pastorals, hunts, and amorous idylls, filled with smiles, sighs, and philosophy, and conversation. The sanctum of the Rococo was the boudoir, its idol was woman, and its mood was caprice.

Of all the varieties of Rococo music, the most representative of the spirit of the times was French keyboard music. It expressed the predilections of Rococo society for elegant and graceful little pieces drenched with showers of ornaments which linger in the air like confetti. This music was not addressed to the public at large; it is out of place in the concert hall, for it was composed for the connoisseurs of the aristocratic salons.

For all their playful tinkling, these delectable French musical bonbons beguiled the musicians of other countries beyond imagination. They looked down upon the little harpsichord pieces, but they saw in them something that they envied — a certain lightness, suppleness, and agility.

The arbiter of this new style was François Couperin, called the Great (1668–1733), who embodied the artistic tenets of his nation. Couperin's numerous clavecin pieces, trio sonatas, and "royal concerts" were perfect expressions of the French musical aesthetics; he wrote and advocated music which would charm, entertain, and perhaps move, but without tears or violent passions.

59

Curarum Levamen

Vignette from Scarlatti's Essercizi per Cembalo, *"for the alleviation of boredom."*

Domenico Scarlatti

THE FREE and easy style of French keyboard music won many adherents. However, the influence of Italian music, always present, was given added weight by the keyboard music of one of the most original minds of the 18th century. Domenico Scarlatti (1685–1757) deepened the rather superficial forms of the French clavecinists by his use of contrasting themes; in so doing, he paved the way for the Classical sonata and its offspring, the Classical symphony.

This greatest of harpsichord virtuosi composed over five hundred short keyboard pieces, originally called "exercises" but now usually referred to as "sonatas." These sonatas, in their radiant and piquant melody, their colorful and exuberant vivacity, their sudden changes from frivolous playfulness to powerful dramatic accents, betray the operatic influence.

Domenico Scarlatti playing the harpsichord. While well known in his time as an opera composer, Scarlatti gained lasting fame by developing the harpsichord sonata.

60

A virginal. A box strung with thirty-eight strings, the virginal could either be placed on a table or held on the lap. Its name comes from virga, the rod equipped with a plectrum which plucked the strings. This instrument produced a tinkling, wispy sound.

From Virginal to Pianoforte

A double virginal or spinet made in the workshop of the Ruckers family of Amsterdam. The keyboard and mechanism could be pulled out and used for outdoor musicals.

The dulcimer. This instrument is still used today in gypsy music. It is played by two sticks with knobbed ends. The player can control loudness by striking the strings lightly or with force.

The orphica, a portable clavichord, whose harplike frame anticipates the shape of the modern grand piano.

The piano forte invented by Cristofori in 1709 had hammers which struck the strings from below, then rebounded to allow the strings to vibrate freely. Although capable of producing the much desired effects of crescendo and decrescendo, Cristofori's idea was not developed until the 1770's.

61

*Musical life at the height of the Rococo period: opera performance in
the French Embassy at Rome, detail from a painting by G. P. Pannini.*

62

Jean Phillipe Rameau:
Thinker, Composer, Performer, and Theorist

THE ART OF Couperin, while universally admired, had a somewhat limited range. The one French composer of the Rococo who excelled in all fields cherished by French thought was Jean Philippe Rameau (1683–1764). Rameau was a profound and keen thinker, a great composer, and a superb performer; his theoretical writings are the foundation of modern musical theory. His instincts drove him toward drama — yet he was unable to sustain a dramatic flow throughout a whole act, for the rationalism of the Enlightenment and the allegorical mythological playfulness of the *style galant* forced him into descriptive excursions and *divertissements*.

Furthermore, Rameau's very logical and scholarly method of work, full of intricate detail, prevented him from abandoning himself to the fluctuating drama. His contemporaries considered him a pedantic craftsman, and indeed, in order to have been the emancipator of the French music drama, this great musician should have had a more poetic nature. Only after a lifetime did he realize that opera could be freed from being a mere musical spectacle — a parade ground of vocal exhibitionism — by restoring the libretto to its true importance. As an old man,

who was the very image of Voltaire, he declared, "If I were twenty years younger I would go to Italy and devote myself to attaining the truth of declamation which should be the sole guide of musicians."

A Fury from Rameau's Zoroastre. *Rameau's ballets were highly successful.*

63

Christoph Willibald Gluck. In his operas dramatic truth was heightened and reinforced by the music. He combined an unflagging persistence with an integrity unimpaired by a good political instinct.

Nicola Piccini — Gluck's adversary in Paris — was a proponent of aria-studded opera while Gluck tolerated no interruption of the dramatic flow by vocal display. Gluck's ideas were victorious.

Christoph Willibald Gluck: Reformer of Opera

THE CRITICS of French opera at the beginning of the 18th century were in full agreement: the music was drowning dramatic action. As Beaumarchais put it, "There is too much music in the musical theater." Rameau's opera *Dardanus* was so dominated by the clamor of the orchestra that one critic remarked, "For three hours the musicians have not even the time to sneeze."

After a lifework spent in all phases of dramatic music, Gluck arrived at the same conclusion when he said that French opera "reeks of music." Christoph Willibald Gluck (1714–1787) was born in the Upper Palatinate, but received his early education and

A performance of Gluck's opera Armide *in Paris. Although his reforms had only a limited success in Vienna, Gluck conquered Paris with the help of his former pupil, Marie Antoinette.*

Gluck's Orpheus and Euridice *achieved fame as a result of its greatness of form, dramatic intensity, and classic proportion.*

musical training in the Jesuit school in Komotau, German Bohemia. He was sent to Italy by a patron, and studied there with Giovanni Battista Sammartini, one of the creators of the early Classical style.

In his youth Gluck wrote examples of the reigning type of Italian opera, in which plot and action were sacrificed to the glorification of *bel canto.* His successes in this genre earned him an invitation to the Haymarket Theatre in London in 1745. Gluck's English excursion was far from successful. He found the Haymarket Theatre a mere shadow of its former excellence, and Handel alienated from opera; these facts made Gluck realize, perhaps for the first time, that Italian opera was declining.

Gluck left London in 1746. *Orpheus and Euridice,* the first opera to embody his new dramaturgical ideas, was written in 1762. The intervening sixteen years were spent in preparing for his reform of Italian opera.

Orpheus was performed in Vienna on October 5, 1762. The opera carried the oldest title in operatic literature, a title that appeared on the bulletin board of every opera theater in Europe; yet Gluck's work became the symbol of the modern music drama.

In *Orpheus* the lifeless figures of the stylized *opera seria* were replaced by sym-bolically simplified and monumental character types reminiscent of the classical tragedy of antiquity. Gluck's ancient heroes were not 17th- or 18th-century princes or kings disguised as gods and heroes; their heroic and sometimes rhetorical pathos had the dimensions and true accents of the tragic greatness of ancient Greece.

It is often said that Gluck relegated music to a secondary place in the drama, that he made it entirely subservient to poetry. On the contrary — in Gluck's operas the music is entirely part of the life on the stage; it carries every scene, every detail, in the drama. What Gluck did was to curtail the da capo aria. In its place, the orchestra is made a factor in the drama, and independent instrumental interludes complete the action as integral parts of the plot.

In *Alceste,* performed in Vienna in 1767, Gluck penetrated even deeper into the problems of the music drama. The musician's task, he felt, was to concentrate on drawing character in music, and to this aim he adhered unswervingly, following the text with profoundly earnest devotion. Gluck's position was clearly stated in the preface to *Alceste:* "I endeavored to reduce music to its proper function, that of seconding poetry by enforcing the expression of the sentiment, and the interest of the situations, without interrupting the action, or weakening it by superfluous ornament."

Gluck's success in Vienna was very modest, because the *opera buffa* monopolized all attention. However, Gluck was not content, and although he was comfortably well off, he moved heaven and earth to gain admittance to the *Opéra* in Paris. When he met difficulties, he turned to his former pupil, the Dauphine Marie Antoinette, who intervened on behalf of her esteemed teacher.

Iphigenia in Aulis, written in French in 1772, was produced in the Académie Royale de Musique on April 19, 1774. *Iphigenia* was followed by French arrangements of *Orpheus, Alceste,* and other trailblazing works. The success of Gluck's operas in Paris was surpassed only by the controversy they created, which ended with the triumph of Gluck. Once vindicated, the composer retired to Vienna to spend his remaining years peacefully, universally admired.

65

The Comic Opera: Popular Musical Entertainment

Rousseau's The Village Soothsayer, *despite the composer's limited musical resources, helped establish the French* opéra comique.

Performance of a comic opera in Paris. This new genre fused elements of the French comic theater and the Italian opera buffa.

GLUCK REPLACED the pseudo-classic tragedy, often overloaded with vapid ornaments, with a music drama that combined depth of feeling, simplicity, and grandeur. A similar reform was achieved in the field of comic opera. Strangely enough the torchbearer of this movement was none other than Jean Jacques Rousseau (1712–1778).

This unique man, who discovered nature, who prepared the Revolution, had also the extraordinary audacity to be a musician. Like everyone else, he was tired of the opera ballet and of the mythological fables with their tedious love affairs promoted or thwarted by a god or a sorcerer; he longed for something that was more in keeping with life. Never more than a half-trained dilettante, Rousseau decided to create a simple folk opera which would contrast with the courtly art of decorative playfulness represented by Lully and his successors — a return to nature in music. He wrote a little

opera, *The Village Soothsayer,* which had a considerable triumph; many composers took it as a model, and even Mozart tried his hand at the genre in his *Bastien and Bastienne.*

Although *The Village Soothsayer* was meagre musically, it introduced a new milieu. Rustic and pastoral scenes, sheepfolds, and peasantry came to replace the mythological and heroic scenes of the *tragédie lyrique* and the ballet-opera. The comic opera received further impetus from the enthusiastic reception of the Italian *opera buffa* in Paris — especially Giovanni Pergolesi's *La Serva Padrona.* The second Paris performance of his work in 1752 created an unprecedented turmoil, the "War of the Buffoons"; musicians and public entered into endless polemics directed by the leading literary men of the times.

The Village Soothsayer combined with the influence of the Italian *opera buffa* to

Giovanni Battista Pergolesi. His opera La Serva Padrona *had a phenomenal success, and helped crystallize the* opéra comique.

Ernest Modeste Grétry, a master of the opéra comique, *who brought Italian vivacity and brilliance into the French form.*

establish a new form of the lyric stage which seemed to be eminently French — the comic opera, whose characteristic traits were good comedy, facility, frivolity, and wit.

The appearance of the comic opera had been accelerated by the pressure exerted on the "illegitimate stage" by the two privileged royal institutions. The Comédie Française prevented any other group's performing spoken plays, and the Académie Royale de Musique insisted on its monopoly to present all works sung from beginning to end. Thus the *théâtre de la foire*, the folk theatre of the market place, was compelled to find theatrical entertainment which did not infringe on either of these monopolies. Elements of this popular art form were grafted upon the Italian *opera buffa* of the Pergolesi type, and as soon as the public's attention was directed to this eminently French form of musical entertainment, the *opéra comique* embarked upon a swift career.

The last great master of the classic *opéra comique* was the Belgian-born André Ernest Modeste Grétry (1742–1813). He had studied in Italy, and had become completely Italianized; but when he returned to France, he heard the comic operas of Philidor and rallied immediately to the cause of French music. He succeeded in transmitting the lifelike vivacity and characterizing ability of the Italian *opera buffa* to the *opéra comique*, and when his admirers called him the French Pergolesi, or the musical Molière, they did not exaggerate his importance. *Richard Coeur de Lion* and *Raoul Barbe-Bleue* are works which exhibit the ideal Gallic mixture of sensibility and comedy.

67

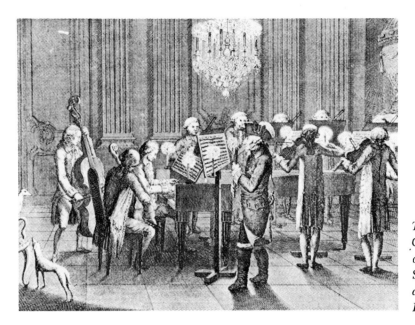

The chamber orchestra of Frederick the Great; Carl Philipp Emanuel Bach is the cembalist, Frederick the flutist. Johann Sebastian Bach's most famous son helped to develop the sonata form later adopted by Haydn and Mozart.

Ensemble Playing Achieves New Nuances: The Mannheim School

THE SEARCH FOR new Classical forms in operas was paralleled by an equally intense desire for new forms in instrumental music. One of the chief sources not only of the form but of the idiom of the Classical instrumental style was the keyboard sonata, notably the sonatas of C. P. E. Bach and his younger brother, Johann Christian Bach.

Carl Philipp Emanuel Bach (1714–1788), Johann Sebastian's second son by his first marriage, was the musician whose personality and initiative consolidated many earlier attempts to create what came to be known as the sonata form. His early piano sonatas make it clear why Haydn and Mozart paid sincere tribute to him. In these sonatas Bach established the musical dialect of the Classical style: symphonic themes, developments of somber intensity, harmonic intricacies, and a disarming humor. In his sonata movements — quick, slow, quick — Bach expounded a new stylistic principle, a new musical logic, coherence, and construction. The continuous expansion of Baroque melody was divided into brief and concise thematic sections, easily comprehensible to the listener.

The new formal elements, first developed in the clavier sonata, set the basic pattern for things to come. The search for new forms was not confined to one city or school. However, in Mannheim, at the court of the Elector Palatine, the new orchestral forms and symphonic techniques were most persistently pursued.

An ardent patron of the arts, Duke Carl Theodor made Mannheim a brilliant center of German cultural life. During the five and a half decades of his reign he spent the enormous sum of thirty-five million florins on artistic and scientific institutions, museums, and libraries, and on his favorite musical establishments, hailed as the best in Europe. Carl Theodor, himself a capable musician, assembled an extraordinary group of players at his court; this group later became known as the Mannheim School, and was made up of musicians engaged from Austria, Bohemia, and Italy. Their leader was Johann Stamitz (1717–1751).

Stamitz merits particular attention for his efforts to achieve a new and perfect orchestral ensemble playing; he was the first German master to break away from the Italian violin schools and develop his own manner of violin and orchestral playing. He trained his musicians individually and drilled them in ensembles. All witnesses agree that the orchestra played together in a faultless ensemble, with uniform bowing and a close observance of dynamic signs and phrasing.

A court orchestra of the late 18th century. These orchestras were grouped into sections of string and wind players, in contrast to previous chamber music ensembles grouped informally around the harpsichord. Early orchestras such as the one shown above consisted of about twenty players led by a violin-bow-wielding conductor.

Duke Carl Theodor, Elector Palatine. He made the Mannheim court a center of art and culture. Its orchestra set a new standard for discipline.

Karl Ditters von Dittersdorf. He wrote symphonies which linked the Mannheim School and the late Classical composers.

Johann Stamitz, leader of the Mannheim School. Although in no sense the inventor of the symphony, he helped develop its over-all form.

Niccolò Jommelli (1714–1774). Born in Naples, he spent fifteen years in Germany experimenting with new orchestral techniques.

As the 18th century advanced, the orchestra expanded. The string choir remained the fundamental body of the orchestra, but its constitutent parts were now clearly differentiated. The wind instruments ceased to be treated as bodies of equivalent standing with the strings; they were required to blend in the scheme of a pliable, unified, yet colorful ensemble. Consequently, such instruments as the trumpet, formerly a melody-bearing instrument, were demoted to the modest place of tonal reserves, called upon to reinforce the sonority whenever needed.

The clarinet, first used in the orchestra by Vivaldi and Rameau, impressed Stamitz when he was in Paris, and he introduced it at Mannheim. Mozart heard the instrument when he visited Mannheim, and he was intrigued by it as he was by the other woodwinds used by Stamitz. "Oh, if we only had clarinets," he wrote to his father. "You can't guess the lordly effect of a symphony with flutes, oboes, and clarinets."

The transverse flute achieved a great success in the 18th century, musically and socially. Whole orchestras were founded with flutes as the dominant instrumental group. The place of the flute in the Classical orchestra was further enhanced in the 1760's when English flute makers added keys to the instruments which eliminated the necessity for cross-fingering, and permitted the player great range and freedom.

Cello

Violin

Bassoon

Double-bass

Flute

Early Classicism still shows a good deal of the delicate feminine touch of the Rococo. Haydn and Mozart, for example, in their early work wrote intimate and playful minuets.

Johann Wolfgang von Goethe in Italy. Together he and Johann Winckelmann, an archaeologist, led the work of rediscovering antiquity.

Classicism: Feeling Disciplined by Form

THE SEARCH for new art forms, spearheaded in music by the Mannheim school, was an intrinsic part of 18-century civilization. In this quest for form, man and art once more returned to the ideal beauty of classical antiquity. Germany was in the forefront of this movement, and the rebirth of the antique through German genius is one of the most important cultural facts of the 18th century.

The 18th century gave life meaning by viewing it from the heights of the eternal ideal. The object of Classical art was to represent man in harmony with nature; drawing on Winckelmann's abstract and stylized conception of Greece, it set its sights on attaining "a noble simplicity and a quiet greatness."

Music as no other art expressed and reflected the tenets of the Classical era. The age mirrored itself with music, which no longer was the servant of particular occasions of worship or of entertainment. Instead, music accompanied life, running parallel with it and always reflecting its riches. Music was the incarnation of the Apollonian art which the century hoped for and which it never quite realized it had found.

The musician who opened the Classical era was part of the new style from its inception to its supreme flowering. Music expressed for him an encompassing love of life seen through a kaleidoscope of wit, humor, joy, and sorrow.

A vignette from Mozart's Complete Works *of a scene from ancient Greece reflects a desire for the classical ideal.*

Haydn's birthplace at Rohrau, Lower Austria. The folk dances and tunes of this region appear in his music.

Haydn as court conductor to the Esterházys. He was required to appear in pigtails and white stockings.

Nicholas Esterházy, Haydn's master for more than thirty years. His castle at Eszterháza was isolated; Haydn said this made him "original."

Franz Joseph Haydn

JOSEPH HAYDN, born on March 31, 1732, in Lower Austria, grew up in a humble but music-loving family. He came to Vienna where his talent was quickly recognized by the members of the aristocracy.

In 1761 Haydn joined his fortunes with those of the Esterházy family. The passion for music of the Esterházy princes made their residence one of the most brilliant of musical centers, particularly after Nicholas Joseph built a magnificent castle which he named Esterház.

Haydn was devoted to Prince Nicholas and realized the unique advantages of his

Haydn conducting from the cembalo his opera The Improvised Meeting at the Esterházy castle (1775). Prince Nicholas's estate had a private theater seating four hundred. Haydn wrote a number of operas for performance during court festivities.

Haydn rehearsing a quartet in the Ester-házy castle.

position. Out of loyalty to his prince the musician refused tempting offers from other courts; but when Prince Nicholas died and his successor disbanded the orchestra and opera, granting Haydn a generous pension, he felt free to undertake artistic tours. Vienna became his home, although his stay there was interrupted by two extended trips to England, in 1791 and in 1794.

Haydn began his career in the midst of the Rococo. In his first works, a dozen or so string quartets, divertimentos, and serenades, there is nothing of the musical construction of the future symphonist. In his search for thematic unity and valid symphonic form Haydn encountered the piano sonatas of C. P. E. Bach. These were a revelation to him, and they account for a new tone in the last few of Haydn's first eighteen quartets. The quartet form appears in clearcut relief, and this very formalism helps Haydn to achieve the mission of music, "to move the heart," as C. P. E. Bach said.

In the next three series of quartets, six to a set, Haydn abandoned the designation "divertimenti"; in these compositions he achieved his characteristic string quartet style. The cyclic form appears with the marked individuality in each of the four

movements. In the last quartet of this period, and especially in the group designated *Opus 20,* the sure and steady stylistic development comes to a halt; and at this point Haydn ceased to compose quartets for a decade to turn his attention to the symphony.

During the next ten years (1771–1781) Haydn experienced, in addition to his own recently acquired mastery in symphonic writing, a powerful influence emanating from the works of his young friend, Mozart. This influence is not expressed in borrowing or imitation, but in a flexibility, a sensitivity, which gave his rhythmic, energetic, and angular musical language added variety. During this decade his ideas ripened and the last remnants of the *style galant* disappeared from his writing.

This new development of Haydn's faculties is exhibited in the symphonies of his middle period. In these works the last vestiges of the operatic origin of the genre, still so obvious in the Italian symphonies and occasionally even in Mozart, are dissolved and converted in a purely instrumental style of great vitality. The better known symphonies of this period are *La Chasse* (No. 73 in the complete edition), *L'ours* (No. 82), *La Poule* (No. 83), *La*

73

Reine (No. 85), and a nameless symphony in G major (No. 88). The titles did not originate with the composer and do not indicate program music; they are merely nicknames derived from rhythms or melodies associated — not without some use of imagination — with such things as the cackling of a hen or the ambling gait of a bear.

With the *Oxford Symphony* (1788), named from its performance in Oxford when Haydn received the honorary degree of Doctor of Music in 1791, the composer arrived at his final period of creative activity. The quartets, symphonies, Masses, and oratorios composed in the next dozen or so years are the works of a consummate master.

In his development of thematic elements Haydn presented only the essential, eliminating everything which had no bearing on the destiny of his subjects. The themes are whittled down to an elemental and plastic simplicity, permitting an unlimited thematic use. Very few composers ever approached this degree of inexorable logic in symphonic construction, and only Beethoven surpassed it.

Musical ideas came freely to Haydn as he extemporized at the piano.

A wax bust of Haydn.

Haydn's genius lived in the instruments; his orchestra is exuberant with life. It is small wonder that he is considered one of the best representatives of German musical culture, of which instrumental music is as typical as vocal music is of the Italian. His operas are not yet sufficiently explored to permit proper judgment of their qualities, but in choral music Haydn can claim a whole chapter to himself.

Haydn's two great oratorios, *The Creation* and *The Seasons*, were written when he was in his sixties, and testify to the undiminished powers of invention of the aged musician. They represent a milestone in the history of the oratorio. The text of *The Creation*, based on a poem by Milton, came from England. Handel had seen this text, but his mighty dramatic fantasy, fond though it was of nature, found it too pale for his liking. Haydn's treatment evoked a great deal of criticism and many smiles. The fact that Beethoven was among those who smiled should not mislead us; for the naïve paint-

Haydn manuscript of his Emperor's Hymn, *beginning "God preserve the Emperor Francis," which became Austria's national anthem. It reappears in the* Emperor Quartet.

ing of lightning and thunder, of rain and snow, of the flow of the river, and of the appearance of the various animals is entirely submerged in the general mood, and blends perfectly with the rest because only the musically feasible was attempted and emphasized.

Following the tremendous success of *The Creation,* the sixty-seven-year-old musician embarked upon the composition of *The Seasons.* Haydn's contemplative nature found an ideal expression in the tableaus that make up this oratorio. Again the occasionally philistine tone may have elicited a smile from the robust composer of *Judas Maccabaeus;* but Haydn's two oratorios do not suffer even when compared to Handel's. The six great Masses composed between 1796 and 1802 are incomparable masterpieces; together with Mozart's similar works, they represent the height of concerted Church music of the Classical era.

Haydn's works will always occupy a definite position in our musical life. Love of life, wholesomeness, clarity, purity of feeling, noble and profound sentiment, inexhaustible humor, and impeccable craftsmanship are the characteristic traits of his art; they should be treasured by us, in whose art these traits appear so seldom.

The Seasons, *written when Haydn was 67, glorifies divine benevolence.*

"Music appeared in the frail boy as a cosmic phenomenon."

Wolfgang Amadeus Mozart

WHENEVER GOETHE spoke of the nature of genius, he mentioned Mozart, who appeared to him as the human incarnation of a divine force of creation. There have been few men in all art in whom genius was so purely, so completely creative, as in Mozart.

Wolfgang Amadeus Mozart was born in Salzburg on January 27, 1756. His life is the most enigmatic example of the history of genius. We need not repeat here the many well-known anecdotes about the abilities of the precocious youth; it seems to the distant observer as though music appeared in the frail child as a cosmic phenomenon. There have been other youngsters who played an instrument adroitly, but at the age of eight Mozart not only was an accomplished piano, organ, and violin player, but had a knowledge of musical composition such as one would expect from a man seasoned in the profession.

He was perhaps the only child prodigy whose peregrinations in various lands did not spoil his taste and originality, but, on the contrary, proved to be highly beneficial. Like Lassus and Handel, he united the musical treasures of all nations of his time. His concert tours gave him a grasp of the essence of the music of his epoch, of the creations of Germany, Italy, and France. He shuffled these elements like a pack of cards, and produced strikingly original and individual music.

Salzburg — a bit of Italy in a German land. Its musical life was modeled after Vienna's, although it maintained its local color.

Mozart's background and heritage prepared him well for his musical mission. The musical life of his birthplace, Salzburg, was modeled after that of Vienna; but it possessed an unmistakable local color. All branches of music were represented in Salzburg by impressive personalities, which had their impact on young Mozart. The most lasting influence, however, was that of the child's father, Leopold Mozart (1719–1787), a noted violinist and a respected composer. His excellent pedagogical insight can be

Christian Bach, consummate master of the style galant, *greatly influenced Mozart.*

Padre Martini, perhaps the century's greatest teacher. He instructed Mozart in counterpoint.

seen in the remarkably rounded musical education he gave his children, drawing on French, Italian, and German compositions both southern and northern. At the age of four to five, Wolfgang played the harpsichord and violin, and, music being his natural language, he started composing virtually before he could write. He was not yet six when his international career began.

This career took him through all the capitals of musical Europe and acquainted him with some of the leading musicians of his time. Of all these, no other composer left such deep marks on Mozart's artistic development as did Johann Christian Bach (1735–1782), the "renegade" son of the Lutheran cantor of St. Thomas's. This German worshipped Italian ideals of beauty and form, and became a consummate master of the *style galant*. When the Mozart family came to London in 1764, Christian Bach divined young Mozart's genius and spent some time in examining and advising him, to the boy's great pleasure.

Mozart's feeling for form and beauty of sound inevitably drove him toward Italian music, and when in December, 1769, father and son went to Italy, the thirteen-year-old musician must have received the Italian experiences as the fulfillment of an instinctive yearning. Daily contact with phenomenal Italian singers soon convinced him that the beauty of music was not to be fully attained in instrumental music, but must use the human voice. Song henceforth dominated his musical imagination, and both the temper of the times and his own dramatic instincts made him turn to the paramount form of vocal composition, the opera.

Still, no matter how deep the Italian impressions were, Mozart did not forget his Austrian homeland, where he discovered in Joseph Haydn another guiding genius for his music. Haydn taught him that in order to achieve perfection in a work of art, one has to live it to the very end. Through Haydn he also discovered that the instruments have souls, and began to compose an avalanche of instrumental compositions: concertos, quartets, sonatas for the new hammer pianoforte, divertimentos, serenades, and symphonies. The richness and variety of this music defies description.

Mozart in 1789. A silverpoint drawing made from life in Dresden by Dora Stock.

MOZART'S INSTRUMENTAL MUSIC

MOZART'S EARLY chamber music reflects the influence of Johann Christian Bach and the Italian masters. It is fresh, unspoiled music, already notable for vivacity of imagination. It is astonishing to see how immediate and effortless, one might say instantaneous, was his orientation as compared with Haydn's careful and conscious sampling and weighing. His early string quartets and symphonies are Italian to the core, singing with abandoned suavity the melodies learned from Sammartini, Tartini, and Christian Bach. The series of chamber music works of the earlier periods are punctuated by a number of divertimentos, which exhibit the same spiritual and technical maturity as the other works, although remaining within their own sphere — and an incomparable sphere it was, the purest music making of all time.

The same animation permeates his other chamber music works. Outside impressions may be strong — as is shown in the dedication of the six quartets to Haydn. Yet Mozart creates an entirely new variety, or rather a new blend, of fugal and homophonic writing. For instance, the finale of the first of this set of six quartets has a fugal beginning, very much like that of the finale of the *Jupiter* symphony, relieved, with the instancy of lightning, by an entirely homophonous passage. Hardly has this change been consummated when the fugato reappears. This time it is enriched with a complementary subject and developed into a double fugue, only to surrender, at the height of its intensity, to an impudent and mischievous little ditty that could have been one of Figaro's asides. This is the creation of a composer who sees life as capable of embracing every mood and climate; no rules of chamber music style apply to this imagina-

First edition of the famous Haydn Quartets. In them Mozart evolved a personal style which he also applied to his symphonies.

in the short interval of six weeks. They represent three totally different moods and aspirations: the E-flat major happy and proud, the G minor passionate and sorrowful, the C major the broadest, the richest, the most classic, expression of Mozart's symphonic art.

The piano was Mozart's first and favorite instrument, and it is only natural that he used it for some of his most personal utterances. Eager to have works of his own available for performance, Mozart experimented a great deal with combining the piano with other instruments. The sonatas for piano and violin; trios for piano, violin, and cello, or piano, clarinet, and viola; quartets and quintets for piano and strings or wind instruments, as well as concertos for piano and orchestra, attest to his search for balance.

Mozart's initial ventures in the area of the concerto were imitations, or even outright arrangements, of piano compositions by masters of the *style galant,* such as Christian Bach. In the second group of his original piano concertos, however, the virtuoso composer found his bearings, and the concerto in E-flat major (K. 271) constitutes one of the original departures in the eighteenth-century concerto literature. Mozart's dislike of patterns made him enter the solo instruments in the second measure as if to announce that henceforth piano and orchestra would be on equal terms. The blending of solo instrument and orchestra is no longer a problem in the later concertos. The composer's fantasy rises to new heights in the D minor concerto. With the very first measures — strangely rumbling muffled basses accompanied by hesitating syncopation in the upper parts — we know that we are in Don Giovanni's abode.

tion and none can be deduced from it; it remains the personal property of its creator.

In the symphony Mozart's style developed but slowly, perhaps because his models, the Italian opera symphony and the post-Stamitz symphony of the Mannheim school, led him into festive rhetoric not flexible enough in mood and technique to suit his nature. He is at his best in the melodious slow movements, and this is understandable considering that his mentor there was Christian Bach, an incomparable melodist. Only after 1782, when Mozart had settled in Vienna, did his symphonic genius come to full fruition. He found flexibility in Haydn, whose symphonic style changed Mozart's outlook and taught him the art of musical logic and continuity.

Within the symphonic pattern, Mozart achieved a singular freedom and depth. The D Major symphony (K. 504), for instance, has an extraordinary introduction, an operatic scene without the vocal parts.

The last three symphonies were composed a year and a half after the D Major,

Figaro measures the room that he will occupy with Susanna after their wedding.

The Count discovers Cherubino in the armchair of the Countess's room.

The Count puts a wreath on Susanna's head during her wedding to Figaro.

Don Juan does not recognize the boundaries of humanity. He clashes with the order of things, and so must perish.

MOZART'S OPERAS

Howemer rich the bounty of Mozart the instrumentalist, the most direct road to an understanding of his art lies through opera. Opera was his preferred medium of musical expression, and in it he recreated the richness of life — both moments of utter tragedy and all-absorbing mirth. Mozart is the supreme master of this art; he has never been surpassed and seldom approached.

At his debut the youthful dramatist found himself faced with many problems. In his vocal works, particularly in his church music, he soon overtook the Neapolitans; but the *opera seria* presented difficulties he was not able to conquer in the first works. *Mitridate* (1770), *Ascanio in Alba* (1771), *Lucio Silla* (1772), and *Scipione* (1772) represent more or less unsuccessful attempts to master the music drama. There is no guiding operatic conviction in them, and they show that their composer was not an Italian, saturated with the traditions of opera. All these had to be learned.

In *Idomeneo* (1781), Mozart found his bearings, if not his definitive style. He parted with the *opera seria* tradition of composing situations created by the plot; he was intent only on psychological characterization of the *dramatis personae*. This opera, now almost forgotten, contains pages that would honor the greatest of operatic composers, and excels especially in individual sketches within the ensembles. The Gluckian tone, which is more noticeable in this work than in any other of Mozart's operas, makes it somewhat stiff and static. After *Idomeneo* Mozart abandoned the *opera seria* forever. He seems to have recognized that an admixture of tragic and comic, embracing the whole range of human emotions, was the atmosphere in which he could best express himself.

Mozart's love of life is at its most harmoniously exuberant in *The Marriage of Figaro* (1786), based on a political satire written by Beaumarchais. The characters in *Figaro* are placed on the stage as life would have thrown them there. In order to realize this picture of life, Mozart turned to the adventurous Venetian, Lorenzo da Ponte (1749–1838), imperial court poet in Vienna

and an able and highly cultivated man of letters. His adaptation of Beaumarchais' original play is a masterpiece of a lyric libretto; he eliminated all political connotations to give Mozart a text that was pure comedy.

Performed on May 1, 1786, in Vienna, *The Marriage of Figaro* was fairly well received and had nine performances. Its fame reached Prague, where it was produced in December to such applause that the management invited the composer to appear in person in the Bohemian capital. For the first time since his childhood, Mozart knew what real success and acclaim meant; but perhaps the most important result of the trip was the incentive to follow *Figaro* with another opera.

When Mozart returned to Vienna, however, he found that *Figaro* had already been shelved. Mozart, whose operas had the reputation of being heavy and difficult, now lost his vogue entirely. His family life and his financial situation left much to be desired. Most of his children had died in infancy, and his wife squandered what little money he earned. Then came the loss of his most cherished friend and counselor: Leopold Mozart died. In this time of sorrow and decline he composed one of the greatest masterpieces of all times, *Don Giovanni*, first performed in Prague on October 29, 1787. Conducted by the composer, the work carried the audience away, the echo of the applause reached the emperor himself, and after many delays *Don Giovanni* was finally produced in Vienna in May, 1788, where it was considered confused and dissonant.

Exuberant love is the subject of this opera. Its hero, the supreme champion of love, perishes tragically because his passions flare beyond the limits of life, challenging the powers that reign beyond it. The passionate and demonic aspects of love are embodied in the hero of the drama, who dominates the work; but love pervades the whole from the lofty and reverent ardor of Don Ottavio to the calculating coquetry of Zerlina. Don Juan, the conqueror, is a truly tragic figure. Like Faust, his only real kinsman, he does not recognize the boundaries of humanity; clashing with the order of things, he is doomed to perish.

Hanswurst, a jester who embodied German comic tastes in his improvised dialogue.

Mozart attending the performance of The Abduction from the Seraglio in Berlin. This Singspiel was the first great German comic opera — light, sunny, pleasing, and filled with wondrous music.

Papageno, a semi-disguised Hanswurst, first played by Schikaneder, the librettist of The Magic Flute.

GENESIS OF *THE MAGIC FLUTE*

THE MEMORY of the years spent in his Austrian homeland before his Italian journeys was never obliterated by Mozart's later experiences. To this heritage of his youth he returned with his opera *The Magic Flute* (1791). Its source is the Singspiel, and we must turn to this art form to gain an understanding of Mozart's last and most enigmatic opera.

The German *Singspiel* appeared in the 1760's, opposing the international opera with a new native and popular form of the lyric stage. The royal and aristocratic vogue for Italian poetry and drama could not stifle the tastes of the public. The popular theater flourished in the teeth of highbrow art, ruled over by a curious traditional figure, *Hanswurst*, a clown who embodied German taste in comedy.

The Emperor, Joseph II, always intent on promoting German culture, realized that the *Singspiel* could become to the Germans what the *opera buffa* was to the Italians. He therefore ordered the establishment of a national *Singspiel* theatre in Vienna. In this theatre, and at the Emperor's command, Mozart's *Abduction from the Seraglio* was produced in 1782 — the first real German comic opera, light, sunny, pleasing, sentimental, fantastic, and filled with wondrous music.

Other ingredients contributed to the growth of the *Singspiel*. The farce, with its theatrical machinery presided over by Hanswurst, was combined with the fairy tale, of which one particular form was the *Zauberoper*, or fairy opera.

An important element underlying Mozart's fairy opera, *The Magic Flute*, was Freemasonry. The lofty ideals of the Masons elicited great admiration not only in the middle classes, but even among the high nobility and members of the imperial house. Among its adherents were Haydn and Mozart, both pious Catholics, but true children of the reign of the high-minded Hapsburg.

Mozart expressed the Masonic credo in *The Magic Flute*. There are the priests of

82

Sarastro explains that hatred cannot exist within the sacred precincts of his temple.

Monostatos the Moor watches the sleeping Pamina. Mozart's music reflects the action.

The Queen of the Night: a personality combining earnestness and fearful sorcery. Stage design by Karl Friedrich Schinkel.

humanity, trying to recruit new followers among men of noble ideas; the realm of the Queen of the Night, opposed to the priesthood of Freemasonry, a province of hatred, sorcery, superstition, and seduction; and finally, the world of those incapable of being elevated to humanism, who must seek and find happiness and goodness in their own simple ways.

Mozart was the greatest musico-dramatic genius of all times. This unique position he owes to a temperament which approached every situation and every human being with absolute objectivity. He did not want to become the German nation's teacher and eulogist, as did Wagner; he did not, like Beethoven, want to reach the highest ideal tone; nor did he, like Handel, want to be God's voice. Every situation and every individual appeared to him as music; his whole conception was purely aesthetic, and music was his language.

As a man Mozart suffered the agonies of a noble soul frustrated and contemptuously humiliated. His life history does not seem to support the popular notion that Mozart is a model and symbol of gracious beauty and harmony. If we look carefully, however, we shall see that everything that seems childlike and simple in Mozart's music is in reality intense and wrought with tragic overtones. He knew that resignation was his lot; he did not step forward to lead the battle. Tamino sings, "Oh dark night, when wilt thou vanish, when will there be light falling on my eyes?" Even at the end, when there was nothing left for him to do but work on a Requiem Mass commissioned by an anonymous patron, death did not permit him to finish this poignant eulogy of the beyond. The voice of the hopeless lover of life broke after the first few measures of the Lacrymosa, and he died in misery on December 5th, 1791, ten weeks after the first performance of *The Magic Flute*.

Mozart's body conveyed to a pauper's tomb. When the hearse left for the cemetery, no one followed the coffin to the grave.

83

18th-Century Concert Life: the Amateur, the Virtuoso, and the Public

AN EVER-INCREASING devotion to music throughout the 18th century brought about a reorientation of concert life and with it the economic position of the composer. While the aristocracy still took a keen interest in performance, it was the music-loving public at large which subsidized the concerts. Mozart was not blessed in this matter. He neither found a permanent princely sponsor, nor was he able to make any substantial sum in extensive concert tours. His economic plight was due to the fact that he lived in a transitional period when the aristocratic sponsorship of music was on the

wane, and the machinery for public concertizing had not yet been so firmly established that it was able to support a musician economically — not even a genius.

Throughout the 18th century, concerts held at aristocratic residences remained inaccessible to the public. However, after the beginning of the century, groups formed among the rising bourgeoisie which sponsored concertizing on a more democratic basis. The English public, in particular, was eager for more music.

Thomas Britton (1643–1714) was perhaps the most curious of the early pioneers

of public music rooms in London. By trade a coal merchant, he spearheaded the movement for public concerts. His business establishment, located in a rented stable, provided the gathering place for notable amateurs and for some of the best musicians of his time, among them Handel. The meetings soon developed into what amounted to regular concerts, for which a subscription price of ten shillings was charged. The great vogue of vocal chamber music in England is reflected in the Noblemen and Gentlemen's Catch Club (1761), with a select membership of royalty and aristocracy complemented by eminent professionals.

The love of music soon reached proportions that cannot be realized by the public of the 20th century. The aristocratic bands played all day, and it was not unusual to perform half a dozen or more symphonies or concertos at one sitting. Concerts took place in all imaginable locations: in inns, taverns, theaters, churches, parks, and in the great halls of the universities.

The English were particularly interested in concert going, and consequently England led in making music available to the general public.

Nicholas Mori, a famous child prodigy, played many concerts during the early 1800's. He eventually became conductor of the Philharmonic Society of London.

Vauxhall Gardens. One of the many London gardens where music was played to large audiences.

1800: At about 30, Beethoven became increasingly aware of his deafness, which forced him to abandon his career as a virtuoso.

1804: Despite adversity, Beethoven composed his symphonies Numbers Three through Eight, the Emperor Concerto, *and his opera,* Fidelio.

1814: His deafness became worse and he began to withdraw from the world. His suffering was further aggravated by family troubles.

1823: An attempt to conduct the revised version of Fidelio *ended in disaster. Notwithstanding his personal tragedy, his spirit rose to new heights in the Ninth Symphony and the Missa Solemnis.*

86

Ludwig van Beethoven

THE MUSIC OF the 18th century seems to flow with serene abandon; yet as the age of aristocratic rule gave way to the age of revolution, as man was nourished by a new vision of the freedom and dignity of the individual, music came to the dawn of a new heroic age.

More than anyone else, Ludwig van Beethoven (1770–1827) lived in this social movement and was carried by it. This humble son of a menial musician discarded the servant's wig and raised his head as the first modern artist who felt himself the equal of princes, profoundly convinced of the dignity of man and fanatically believing in freedom. His music echoes this personality tenfold.

With the phenomenal success of the child Mozart still vivid in the memory of the musical world, Johann van Beethoven decided to turn the unmistakable musical talents of his son Ludwig to profitable employment. At the age of eight the child appeared in public as a pianist, and three years later he was taken on a short concert tour. His instruction was entrusted to rather insignificant musicians who happened to be in Bonn; then in 1779, Beethoven came under the influence of a well-trained and ex-

The Beethoven House in Bonn, Germany, where the composer was born on December 16, 1770.

perienced musician, Christian Neefe (1748–1798), who divined the youth's exceptional talents and in an article published in 1783 predicted his career as successor to Mozart.

A first visit to Vienna in 1787 was interrupted by Beethoven's mother's death; in 1792, Beethoven made Vienna his permanent home. His hopes of studying with Mozart had been shattered by the latter's death in the previous year; thus he approached the other great leader of the Viennese school, Haydn. The old and the young master could not see eye to eye. Haydn was not made to be a teacher, while Beethoven was a born antagonist.

Luckily the same aristocracy which had sponsored the older composers now took Beethoven under its wing. But the young musician was no longer a favored servant, like Haydn; Beethoven was received in the aristocratic palaces as an honored guest. Furthermore, there was something in his music which was incompatible with the atmosphere of the aristocratic salons, a certain heretofore unknown ampleness of tone and gesture that broke through the circle of the privileged few to appeal to the multitude.

Beethoven in the streets of Vienna. Eccentric in appearance, he was once mistaken for a vagabond.

87

On March 29, 1795, Beethoven appeared for the first time before the Viennese public, playing his Piano Concerto in B-flat. In the same year his *Opus* 1, three piano trios, appeared, followed in the next year by three piano sonatas. His creative activity continued to expand, and in the next few years he wrote the piano sonatas of *Opera* 5, 7, 10, 13 (the *Pathétique*), 24, and 26; six string quartets; the septet; two more piano concertos; the First and Second Symphonies; the ballet, *Prometheus;* and the oratorio, *The Mount of Olives.*

The next five years brought forth another miraculous harvest of great works — symphonies, sonatas, trios, and quartets. In acknowledgement of his growing reputation, on December 22, 1808, Beethoven gave a big concert in the Theater an der Wien,

presenting to the packed auditorium his G major Piano Concerto, parts of the C major Mass, and the Fifth and Sixth Symphonies, as well as the Fantasy for Piano, Orchestra, and Chorus, *Opus* 80.

Although Beethoven's creativity increased, he withdrew more and more from his friends. His personality was such that he easily felt disappointed and embittered, and was often harassed by suspicions — feelings greatly intensified by the gradual loss of his hearing, the first symptoms of which manifested themselves in his late twenties. In the next decade it became apparent that his ailment was incurable; and in his last years he was totally deaf. Thus, at a time when his fame had spread all over Europe, Beethoven avoided the public and lived almost like a recluse.

A soirée in the palace of Count Rasumowsky, a Russian nobleman. Rasumowsky, a musician himself, had his own quartet which he placed at Beethoven's disposal for his chamber music.

Fidelio, *or* Married Love, *was Beethoven's only opera. Produced in Vienna in 1805, it had an unfavorable reception. He revised it often during the ensuing years, revisions which included compressing it into two acts.*

Theater an der Wien where Fidelio *was first produced. The opera was withdrawn after three performances. The three* Leonore *overtures are part of Beethoven's attempts to revise* Fidelio.

The misery of his physical condition, and the endless annoyances caused by an ungrateful nephew whom he treated like his own son, could make the man despair but not the composer. The last great piano sonatas, *Opera* 101, 106, 109, 110, and 111, the Diabelli variations and Bagatelles, and the cello sonata, *Opus* 102, opened his last stylistic period. Then two colossal creations, the Ninth Symphony and the *Missa Solemnis,* materialized from among many plans for large oratorios, operas, and symphonies. By this time the public had ceased to know the composer, although his name was a symbol in Vienna. Once more, however, Beethoven experienced the esteem and affection of the Viennese at the first performance of the Ninth Symphony (1824) before a deeply moved audience. After long and intense sufferings, he died on March 26, 1827.

Beethoven's room, with his hammerklavier. Beethoven's interest in the piano sonata was revived in 1818 when English admirers presented him with a Broadwood piano.

Beethoven's Instrumental Music

THE CENTRAL THOUGHT in Beethoven's works, even his works for individual instruments, is symphonic. Sonatas, quartets, and symphonies all belong together stylistically; all of them are dominated by the dramatic dualism of the classical sonata form.

The keyboard sonata had become a flexible and dramatic medium in the works of C. P. E. Bach; his work in this genre was further developed by Mozart, the first real virtuoso on the pianoforte, which had supplanted the harpsichord.

The piano sonata reached its culmination, however, in Beethoven's thirty-eight works in this form. Beethoven started out using the traditional forms and idioms, but he soon exhausted the classical piano sonata and did not hesitate to enrich it with his own variants. The genre remained Beethoven's most personal medium and one in which he experimented to his heart's content.

In his first quartets Beethoven did not simply continue where Haydn stopped. Mastery like Haydn's comes only after lifelong development, and Beethoven had to evolve his own quartet style. The road was not easy and entailed a great deal of experimentation, reflected in a variety of thrusts into the peripheries of chamber music. Beethoven's quartet style, enriched by a polyphonic ensemble technique learned from Haydn, reached its first summit around 1807 with the completion of the third Rasumowsky Quartet in C. After the Quartet in F Minor (1810), Beethoven found it was no longer possible to continue in this style, and a pause became necessary. For a dozen years or so, he wrote no string quartets. Then, during his last period of creativity, he once more returned to this medium, expressing in his last quartets of 1824–1826 his innermost spiritual experiences. In these last works Beethoven transcended the normal bounds of musical form; dimensions of form are eliminated, and pure music triumphs over construction.

90

Beethoven composing the Pastoral Symphony: *scene at the brook. He loved nature passionately and remarked to Schindler that the birds in the forest near Heiligenstadt had helped him compose the* Pastoral.

A portrait sketch of Beethoven by Moritz von Schwind, who grew up in Vienna and undoubtedly had seen Beethoven in the city.

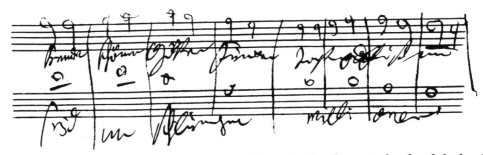

Sketch for the theme of the choral finale of the Ninth Symphony.

Beethoven's orchestral music reached horizons unknown before his time. The Third Symphony especially is one of the incomprehensible deeds of art — the greatest single step made by an individual composer in the history of the symphony and in the history of music in general. This should not be interpreted as belittling the other symphonies; the *Eroica* simply dwarfs them all in its boldness of conception, breadth of execution, and intense logic of construction. Beethoven himself never again approached this feat of fiery imagination; he wrote other, perhaps greater, works, but he never again took such a fling at the universe.

The most convincing, the most miraculously concentrated, symphonic structure in all musical literature is Beethoven's Fifth Symphony, the fulfillment of the symphonic ideal. The first movement of the Fifth Symphony is built on a theme consisting of four notes supplied by two tones, surely the minimum for a musical theme. The hammering strokes of the orchestra seize us with irresistible force. There is no letdown in their progress, and the inexorable logic of thematic development, which is interrupted by the plaintive little recitative of the oboe, plunges again into the headlong turmoil which ceases only at the end of the movement. The same degree of concentration characterizes the scherzo of the Ninth Symphony. It is incredible that these terse ideas can develop into the vastness of a symphonic movement; and yet they are not merely the point of departure, they are the essence, the governing force itself, of the symphonic development.

The great Ninth Symphony, despite its choral finale, is orchestrally conceived throughout. The sufferings and trials of humanity, expressed in the first three movements with the greatest of intensity, are conveyed to us by orchestral means. The chorus which joins the orchestra during the fourth movement merely supplements it, and the disposition of the finale is fully determined in the purely orchestral introduction and set of variations which precede the vocal entry.

During the first performance of the Ninth Symphony (1824), Beethoven was not aware of the public's applause until he was led to the front to see the clapping hands.

91

Beethoven (carrying basket) in a courtyard in the village of Heiligenstadt, where he spent some of his summers.

Like the Ninth Symphony the *Missa Solemnis* is a work of enormous proportions, both physical and spiritual, reminiscent of the great Baroque composers. As Bach did in his B minor Mass, Beethoven left behind all churchly thought. Beethoven himself was aware of this quality in his *Missa*, and even recommended it be performed in the concert hall. This did not, however, imply an abandonment of the original purpose of the work. What he really wanted was to have this Mass, which he considered his supreme achievement, available to Protestants as well as Catholics. The *Missa Solemnis* is planned and fused from the first to the last tone. Wagner recognized this when he called it "a purely symphonic work bearing the true stamp of Beethoven's mind."

We still do not realize the tremendous impact Beethoven's music had on the succeeding generations. Instrumental music was under his spell for the rest of the century, and there is still no department of music that does not owe him its very soul. He endowed pure instrumental music with the most intense and expressive dramatic accents — the sonatas, quartets, and symphonies are dramas, even if they have nothing to do with the stage — and he created a heroic style which unleashed subjective forces unknown to his Classical predecessors.

But although Beethoven opened wide the doors, he did not enter the new halls; he remained a true Classicist to whom force was form. Beethoven's whole art is the triumph of power over material; he is Janus-faced, looking at the same time backward, expressing the ultimate apotheosis of Classicism, and forward, beckoning to the future, a guide and teacher for the nineteenth century.

Beethoven composing the Missa Solemnis. *This is the work of a profoundly gentle soul, who yet is willing to dare a fervent abandonment.*

Life mask of Beethoven taken by Franz Klein.

Beethoven's funeral procession.

Vienna was a magnet which drew musicians from all countries of Central Europe.

Vienna: Musical Capital

VARIOUS FACTORS MADE Austria the center of the Classical school. For one thing, the easy-going disposition and flexibility of the southern Germans welcomed the international atmosphere of the cultural life of the old Austrian Empire. Many musical styles were mingled in the music of the Viennese school: English keyboard music, French comic opera, and German *Singspiel* all found their way there, uniting French *sensibilité,* Italian *dolcezza,* and Austrian *Gemütlichkeit.*

Furthermore, the popular music played in Vienna's amusement parks, such as the Prater and Grientzig, also had a marked influence on the Viennese style, adding elements of freshness and unaffected grace. The musical vitality in the works of the Viennese school was nourished on the tunes of the city's street singers, balladeers, and dancebands, and echoed rhythms of the Austrian, Bohemian, and German peasants. The composer who most perfectly fused these two elements of the Viennese style — the cosmopolitan and the popular — was Franz Schubert.

In the Prater, Vienna's amusement park, the crowds were entertained by singers and instrumentalists.

94

Serenading at night was a popular pastime in Vienna. Mozart's Haffner Serenade and Schubert's Octet reflect this night music.

Street musicians playing in a Vienna courtyard. These groups kept alive many folk tunes. In 1819 Beethoven wrote his Mödling Dances for a group like this one.

There were many Hungarian gypsy orchestras in Vienna; the works of Schubert, Haydn, and Beethoven echo their music.

As a youth, when he already had begun to compose Lieder and symphonies.

In his mid-twenties, about 1822, after he wrote his Eighth Symphony — the Unfinished.

Schubert's appearance was unprepossessing. Detail from a sketch by Schwind.

A wash drawing of Schubert by Wilhelm August Rieder done in 1825. This drawing was acclaimed by Schubert's friends as being his most lifelike portrait.

Franz Schubert:
Classicism and Romanticism

Beethoven exclaimed, after perusing some songs by Schubert, "Truly he has the divine spark." This divinely gifted musician, under whose hands every pebble became harmony, had a short and simple life. Born in Vienna in 1797, Franz Peter Schubert received his first musical education from his father. Perhaps the most important factor in Schubert's life and education was the love of music in his home, where playing chamber music was a daily event. His compositions often have the stamp of music written to be played for one's own enjoyment.

Schubert's development was decisively influenced by his early acquaintance with a group of highly cultivated young poets and writers who introduced him to the ideas of Romanticism. After teaching school for a while, Schubert abandoned all ties with ordinary middle-class life, and without any regular income lived mainly on the good will of his friends. These friends were generous and faithful; but their generosity was sharply limited by their own modest means.

Schubert's precocity is well illustrated by the compositions of the years 1814–1816, when he wrote some of the gems of the song literature, among them *Gretchen at the Spinning Wheel* and the *Erl King*. Most of his early instrumental works were written for the excellent Viennese dilettante groups, and he himself was welcome in well-to-do music lovers' homes as a good pianist, especially notable for his improvisations of Viennese dances.

In 1823 his frail health forced him to enter a hospital; he was still ailing when, later that year, he wrote the song cycle *The Fair Maid of the Mill*. The next five years were spent in perpetual struggle to obtain a position conducting. His financial position deteriorated, and in his last year of his life, his friends had to arrange a benefit concert of his own compositions, which netted him some much-needed money. Schubert died on November 19, 1828, in his thirty-first year. His last wish, to be buried near Beethoven, was fulfilled.

His contemporaries had no idea of Schubert's significance. His most important works were either unknown to them or not properly understood. The parochial romanticism of the early 20th century, which put together operettas out of melodies plucked from his songs and symphonies (*Blossom Time*), regarded him as a prodigal melodist, an innocent Biedermeier figure spending his time in merry company in the Viennese cafés, quite at a loss as to what to do with his inexhaustible invention.

An excursion by Schubert and his friends to the suburbs of Vienna. These outings were full of songs, dances, and musical fun.

The song cycle The Fair Maid of the Mill. Schubert's song cycles have been called distilled operas performed without a stage.

The Wanderer, one of Schubert's most popular songs. Some of its thematic material was used in the Wanderer Fantasy.

An evening musicale at the home of Josef von Spaun. Schubert, at the piano, accompanies Johann Michael Vogl, an excellent singer and an enthusiastic apostle of Schubert's songs. This sketch is by Moritz von Schwind, another distinguished member of the Schubert circle.

The song writer in Schubert was uninhibited and original from the very beginning; but the instrumental composer had to struggle for clarity. The earlier piano sonatas are diffuse and restless, although there are passages of bewitching beauty. On the other hand, the lyric piano pieces, impromptus, and moments musicaux show Schubert at his best. Every one of these pieces is an exquisite lyric confession of a musical poet.

In chamber music and symphony Schubert was confronted with the towering figure of Beethoven. In his Second Symphony in B-flat the youngster attempted to emulate the large Beethovenian gesture, as he did in the Fourth Symphony, more tragic in intention than in outcome. It is true that in his chamber music and in his symphonies Schubert did not always follow the symphonic lineage of Haydn and Beethoven, for instead of concentrating on the exploitation of a terse symphonic idea he often reached with both hands into the inexhaustible treasure chest of his melodic invention; but he could still muster enough discipline to prevent diffusion.

Schubert's greatness is made obvious by the fact that the so-called *Unfinished Symphony* was written in 1822, in the immediate vicinity of Beethoven's Ninth. Here is a composer inspired by Beethoven who dares to follow the Titan to dizzy heights, and return with a work which can be placed next to those of Beethoven without paling. The sentimental idea derived from the youthful death of the composer that this symphony was his last, is incorrect. In reality, at least two great symphonies followed (one of them unhappily lost), and the only reason for Schubert's not finishing the Eighth Symphony must have been that his mood was completely exhausted. Far from regarding it as a magnificent torso, we should treasure the B minor Symphony as a consummate work of art, free from all formalistic restrictions.

The Erl King, *a song based on Goethe's ballad about the legend that whoever is touched by the King of the Elves must die.*

99

The C Major Symphony was Schubert's last, and also the last mighty classical symphony. What magnificent and truly symphonic élan, and what a wealth of development from the heroic, utterly classic, symphonic theme! The finale of this symphony moved Schumann to comment on its "heavenly length": "How refreshing is this feeling of overflowing wealth! With others we always tremble for the conclusion, troubled lest we find ourselves disappointed."

In his chamber music, as in his symphonies, Schubert, despite the Beethovenian magnet to which he was drawn, was able to reconcile Classicism and Romanticism. In the *D Minor Quartet,* with its variations on the familiar song *Death and the Maiden,* Schubert resurrected this favored medium of the Classical composers in all its glory. Schubert was the composer in whom the Beethovenian lineage ended; symphony and chamber music declined after him and did not find another true disciple until Brahms.

Schubert's greatest contribution to music lay in his treatment of the *Lied,* the German Romantic song. In his over six hundred *Lieder,* he consciously gave the purely musical elements, such as harmony and instrumental accompaniment, an equal importance with poem and melody.

Few musicians' works convey such an impression of the outdoors as do Schubert's. Nature inspired a large part of his lyric output. In his wanderings in and around Vienna, in Upper Austria, Styria, and western Hungary, he picked the wild flowers of folk music and presents them to us, arranged in wonderful bouquets, in his songs and dances.

The Concert, *by Moritz von Schwind. The painter, a personal friend of Schubert, made many drawings of the Schubertian circle. Schwind appears in the center of the picture, turning the music for the lady pianist. Schubert is third from left in the chorus.*

The Liedler, *a drawing by Moritz von Schwind.*

100

Book Four

MUSIC IN THE
ROMANTIC
ERA

All Romanticism seems youthful compared to Classical maturity. Novalis created the symbol of Romanticism, the unattainable blue flower.

Romantics adored nature and lived wedded to it.

The Romantics were the poets of the apotheosis of love.

102

Its longing for the far away, the infinite, tinged all Romantic art with melancholy.

The Mood of Romanticism

BOTH BEETHOVEN and Schubert stand at the end of the Classical period facing the dawn of a new era. In Beethoven Classicism became Romantic; in Schubert Romanticism became Classic. Schubert was not in search of the unattainable. Rather, he reveled enthusiastically in attained perfection. His songs and symphonies, although saturated with emotion, are firmly anchored to reality.

Schubert's personal fate, however, has come to symbolize Romanticism. He died young; and all Romanticism seems youthful compared to Classical maturity. Romanticism was actuated by the ideals of youth, friendship, and subjective universalism. Romantic idealism was dedicated to the whole of humanity, and to the whole of art. The fusion of all the arts was its aim: its poets painted, its painters made music. Literary ideas were at the bottom of much of its music; the German novelist, Jean Paul, avowedly tried to achieve musical effects in his writings, a fact which made Robert Schumann declare, "I learned more counterpoint from Jean Paul than from my music teacher."

The urge for union is the essence of Romanticism; and love and friendship — forms of association — were its chief subjects. The Romantics were the poets of the apotheosis of love and the most passionate champions of friendship. Their attempt to reduce everything into unity, to find all ideas kindred, was a direct reaction to the cool and deliberate articulation of the Enlightenment. The Enlightenment separated and delimited; Romanticism bound and united. Soul and matter, spirit and nature, melted into love and into a love of the infinite.

To the Romanticists nature was revelation, the expression of human experience; Romanticism abandoned itself to nature and lived wedded to it. Hölderlin and Novalis, Byron and Shelley, Schubert and Weber, all sang of and thought with nature, unlike the men of the Enlightenment who loved in nature only the idyllic. The Romantic was filled with nature, and immersed himself in it.

Poetry and music offered the best expressions for this pantheistic philosophy. However high the Romantic spirit surged in its poetry, though, music was recognized as the true language of the movement. No other art could express the longing for the infinite, no other art could bring men into such close contact with the universe; music, for the Romantics, was the symbol of infinite unity.

103

Romanticism had many ties with the Revolution. The Revolution had emancipated the middle classes, and as a result cultural leadership had become imbued with the petty bourgeois spirit, with all its desire for practicality and comfort.

The Biedermeier style was the product of middle-class leadership. The bases for the Biedermeier style were a bourgeois simplification of the Classical forms of the Enlightenment and a retreat from the pathos of Romanticism — a tired flight into quietude, modesty, and simplicity. There is a remarkable telescoping of the real and the desired in the Biedermeier world picture; it feigns an ever-happy, shadowless existence, an eternal, radiant Sunday. There is no dust on its objects, and no concern or solicitude on the faces of the people; order and satisfaction are everywhere. It was not that the artists of this era did not realize the vicissitudes of life; they knew them well, but they took refuge in the illusion of this seeming fairyland in order to escape the outside world.

Biedermeier art stressed cosiness and comfort. In music, piano playing and family chamber music were paramount, followed by romances and songs.

Though he suffered from consumption, Weber was a man of great energy and aristocratic bearing. His poetic air made him the image of the Romantic composer.

German Romantic Opera: Carl Maria von Weber

THE OPERAS OF Carl Maria von Weber (1786–1826) were an early expression of German Romanticism. Appearing in the midst of the final splendor of the Classical symphony, Weber was a Romantic of the purest water, entirely free of formal doubts and scruples and profoundly convinced of the righteousness of his cause. He created the musical Romanticism of the forest, the most Germanic of Romantic moods. Weber's operas marked the victory of the German Romantic opera over the French revolutionary and empire opera which had been admired and followed by all other early nineteenth-century composers, including Beethoven. What Mozart and Beethoven were not able to achieve, Weber, a man of infinitely more modest talents, accomplished: a closer relationship between the German people and German music.

As a conductor Weber was a stern taskmaster. He insisted on perfection in every detail and held separate rehearsals for strings and wind instruments.

Der Freischütz, Weber's most celebrated opera, tells the
story of a huntsman who sells his soul to the devil in
order to obtain six magic bullets. Its music evokes the
terror and mystery of a haunted forest.

106

When Mendelssohn visited Goethe in 1821, the famous poet-philosopher accepted this precocious boy on terms of equality.

Felix Mendelssohn at the age of eleven. He had already composed a number of pieces for the piano.

Felix Mendelssohn: Disciplined Romanticist

FELIX MENDELSSOHN BARTHOLDY (1809–1847) was the grandson of the great Jewish philosopher Moses Mendelssohn and son of a wealthy banker and of a mother of exceptional culture and refinement. His family's wealth and solicitous care provided him with the best teachers available in Berlin. Having at his disposal every combination of ensembles in the regular house concerts, the seventeen-year-old composer created works of incredible maturity and genius, among them the radiant octet for strings and the bewitching overture to Shakespeare's *Midsummer Night's Dream*. He learned to appreciate Bach, and was responsible for a performance of the *St. Matthew Passion* in 1829, the first of other notable premières and revivals which made Mendelssohn the great authority in the thirties and forties to whom composers and scholars appealed for advice and encouragement.

Endowed with great melodic gifts and with a craftsmanship given to few, this remarkable and many-sided musician is usually remembered as the sentimental composer of *Songs Without Words;* yet he was by no means a devotee of the soft and sentimental tone that characterized this period. He was intelligent enough to know that glowing passions and profound emotions were not in his make-up; therefore the emotional content in his works is carefully articulated and toned down. His is a gentle kind of well-organized Romanticism, tamed by a

A drawing by Mendelssohn showing St. Thomas' Church and St. Thomas' School at Leipzig, where Bach worked. The revival of Bach's music by Mendelssohn influenced composers for generations after.

sound bourgeois attitude. To Mendelssohn's circle, the enjoyment of music was *plaisir*, and good music was *charmante*. He adored elegant fluency and was somewhat terrified by the force embodied in the Ninth Symphony.

It was with this disposition that Mendelssohn approached the greatest problem of Romanticism: form. Although he understood the meaning of the Classical sonata-symphony, in his hands the Classical spirit became a notable gesture, acquired but not assimilated. His plan to reconcile Classical construction with Romantic content was doomed from the beginning, for although his wonderfully polished and fluent writing lent itself admirably to any type of construction, the lack of conflict and the tight rein give this highly refined and cultivated music a bourgeois, and at times a sentimental, air. There can be no question that many of Mendelssohn's works lack depth. A certain sober clarity permeates his music — not the clarity implicit in mood and conviction, but that imposed by the organizing mind.

Manuscript of Mendelssohn's most popular melody, On Wings of Song, *the epitome of Romantic love in music.*

The oratorio Elijah (Elias *in German) was performed one year before Mendelssohn's death. This work proved particularly popular in England.*

108

Mendelssohn playing the organ, a drawing by the composer made during his visit to Heidelberg. His contemporaries considered him a fine organist.

Felix Mendelssohn — a deft, amiable, and polished man and musician. Touched by the Romantic spirit, he preserved the purity of the Classical style.

While we cannot help noting these limitations in Mendelssohn's music, which were largely due to his nature and his social philosophy, he nonetheless gave us much that fills us with quiet enjoyment and admiration. Two of his symphonies enjoy undiminished popularity: the A minor, called *Scottish,* and the A major, called *Italian.* Both are distinguished by freshness and wonderful orchestral coloring, yet they are entirely compatible with symphonic thought.

The fine scherzo of the *Italian Symphony* leads us to Mendelssohn's most original and personal creations, the fairy scherzos. One of the most entrancing of these is found in the *Midsummer Night's Dream* music. In it Mendelssohn takes us into the very center of the fairyland of Romanticism. His is, however, not a mysterious or fearful fairyland; in its glens the gnomes and elves play around merrily, full of good will. After Mendelssohn came a legion of imitators who made the fairies dance; but no one else was able even remotely to match his shadowy lightness. He also composed some of the finest chamber music of the Romantic era.

Robert Schumann, as a youth. He devoted himself to Romantic literature, and thought of becoming a poet. Only later did he decide music was his true mission.

An early daguerreotype of Schumann, taken in 1850. His contemporaries described his face as soft and round, with an invariable expression of ineffable pain clouded by reverie.

The house at Zwickau in which Robert Schumann was born in 1810. His father was a publisher and translator, which explains Robert's literary interests.

A musical gathering at the house of Professor Justus Thibaud, Schumann's mentor at the University of Heidelberg.

Robert Schumann

THE CLASSICAL PERSONALITY was firm and undivided; the Romantic had a double character, at the same time vehement and strong and gentle and poetic. The Romantic ego was eternally reforming; for that endless striving with itself is its very soul.

Robert Schumann (1810–1856) united in his person the richness of the poetic imagination of the Romantic with the sensitive reaction of the musician. He endeavored to solve the riddle of life by music, and two of his fictional creations, Florestan and Eusebius, embody the dual aspects of the Romantic personality. The pursuit of the problems and secrets of life was indispensable to him; his imagination was kindled by the dusk and the night, by everything mysterious, puzzling, and ghostly.

The tragedy of Schumann's life lay in his inability to reconcile the tenets of Romanticism with the demands of Beethoven's Classical form. His heroic attempt was doomed to failure. In his hands the Classical symphony and sonata disintegrated, and he treated the sonata form as simply a framework to hold the release of emotions within bounds.

Schumann's First Symphony, written in the happiest period of his life, sparkles with life and optimism, and truly deserves its title, *Spring Symphony*. It was written in an uncommonly short time, and is relatively free of the obstinate rhythmic patterns and dearly-won connecting links that characterize Schumann's larger instrumental works. All of Schumann's symphonies contain much beautiful music, but, in true Romantic fashion, their beauty is in their details.

The rhapsodic mood of Romanticism is better expressed in smaller forms, in the rippling tones of the piano, the velvety smoothness of the human voice; this fact is evident in Schumann's songs and piano pieces, which are works fully the equals of the greatest creations of the past. The lyric "musical moment," though largely the creation of Mendelssohn, appears most typically in Schumann's cyclic pieces — *Kinderszenen, Kreisleriana, Carnaval;* every piece in these cycles is complete and independent in itself, and each projects a different mood, here frolicking, there lapsing abruptly into earnest meditation.

Like the other Romanticists of this era, Schumann was master of the song, in which he told of his own love in a lyricism of unsurpassed sensitivity. In 1840, when he was finally united with Clara Wieck, he wrote *Myrthen,* the Eichendorff song cycles, his settings of Heine's *Liederkreis* and *Dichterliebe,* Rückert's *Liebesfrühling,* Chamisso's *Frauenliebe,* and a number of others, a bounty unparalleled in the annals of music. Schumann had a marked penchant for literature, and no matter how purely lyrical his songs, they give us, especially in the cycles, a picture of the development of mental experiences. His piano has an intimate relationship to both text and voice, often contributing more to the expression of the mood than the voice itself.

The Romantic composers and poets always sang; all their poems are texts to be set to music, and the melodies hover about them. No one, however, proved more convincingly than Schumann that the soul of Romanticism is music.

The titlepage, designed by Ludwig Richter, for Schumann's cycle Songs for the Young.

Kapellmeister Kreisler was a picturesque virtuoso from a novel by E. T. A. Hoffmann. Schumann immortalized him in his Kreisleriana, *a cycle of piano pieces dedicated to Chopin.*

112

Schumann's study in Düsseldorf. In spite of growing discontent and anxiety, Schumann created here such inspired work as the Rhenish Symphony *and* the Fantasy-Pieces for Piano, Opus 111.

ROBERT AND CLARA

Clara Wieck in 1836, at seventeen. She was already a piano virtuoso. In this year a romance began between Clara and Robert Schumann, but they were only able to marry after a long legal struggle with Clara's obstinate and possessive father, Robert's teacher, Friedrich Wieck.

Despite its many problems, the marriage of Robert and Clara Schumann was glowing and happy.

Frédéric Chopin. The nationalist Slavic element in his work passed into the mainstream of European music. His polonaises reflected the longing he felt for his native Poland.

Frédéric Chopin: The Poet of the Piano

SCHUMANN'S CELEBRATED manifesto of 1831 hailed Chopin as one of the heroes of Romanticism. Born in 1810, the son of a French father and a Polish mother, Frédéric Chopin was one of those youthful giants who appear on the scene of musical history with a finished personal art. His great talent soon drove him toward the centers of musical life; in 1829 and 1830 he was acclaimed in Vienna and Munich, and then, like many other Polish emigrés, he settled down in Paris. He became the idol of the distinguished Parisian salons and a much-sought-after piano teacher and performer. Surrounded by fame and a brilliant society, his death was hastened by a stormy love affair with the imperious and domineering George Sand; after they parted in 1847 he succumbed to tuberculosis, and died in the prime of his life in 1849.

Chopin was one of the creators of the Romantic musical idiom. Among his mature works there is not one that depends on traditional forms or devices, for he made his own musical universe. This universe, more than that of any other Romantic composer, is the complete antithesis of the Classic, especially Beethovenian, world. Classical musical architecture with its balanced form is foreign to Chopin's art, which is capricious, arbitrary, always fascinating, and characteristic down to the smallest detail. The elements of Chopin's music are not subjected to a higher law of form; the enchanting melodies and multicolored harmonies achieve their own fantasy-like forms which admirably reflect the nature of this music.

George Sand, author and feminist, and Chopin's mistress. They met in 1836. Her protective love made the years they spent together inspired ones for Chopin.

Chopin was able to write his melodies only with heart-rending effort: "He would shut himself in his room for days, modifying a bar a hundred times."

All his life Chopin moved in society's upper strata. His playing was ideal for intimate musicales, but too delicate for large concert halls.

A daguerreotype of Chopin, taken in the late 1840's. His break with George Sand marked the end of his creativity, and he remained ill until his death in 1849.

Chopin's death mask, by Jean Baptiste Clesinger.

Chopin's free constructions and his melodic and harmonic idiom supplied the most important elements of Romantic music. Without him the music of the second half of the 19th century is hardly imaginable. His originality is so compelling, every one of his ideas and phrases is so uniquely his own, that perhaps no other composer can be so quickly identified. The range of his sentiments is astonishingly wide, running from light, almost ethereal, melancholy to scintillating fireworks and hymnic exaltations.

Chopin was the first great composer in whose music the Slavic element came strongly to the fore, and this element passed from his work into the mainstream of European music. His Polish blood throbs with particular vigor in his warlike polonaises with their boldly arching melodies. The knightly mazurkas glow with fiery gestures; sweet languor and coquetry live in the waltzes. Besides these dance forms, Chopin wrote fantasies, scherzos, and ballads, impromptus, preludes, and sonatas — lyric effusions of a sometimes demonically mysterious, sometimes enticing and cajoling, but always warm and gracious heart. The spirituality which he made a universal language through his lyricism celebrated its highest triumphs in the sparkling études; the nocturnes are the dreams of his solitude, expressing the deepest longings of a man outwardly spoiled by good fortune but in reality, like many of his Romantic contemporaries, a virtuoso of suffering.

Chopin's hands were rather small, yet their suppleness made them ideally suited to piano playing.

The Search for the Spectacular: Grand Opera in France

THE WORKS OF Mendelssohn, Schumann, and their Romantic brethren gave Germany undisputed leadership in the field of instrumental music. The French Romantic movement, no less pronounced, found its rather ostentatious expression in the supreme spectacle of grand opera.

The children of the men of the Revolution and the Napoleonic era — men who had witnessed in their youth the horrors of the upheaval and the glory of the Empire — looked for an image to reflect their exuberant age. The sons wanted to make the same gestures in their private life that their fathers had made on the barricades or on the battlefields. Reduced to inactivity by historical events, the French nation spent the two decades between 1825 and 1845 in imagining what could no longer be achieved. Since it could no more live the great adventures, it read about and listened to them. In this atmosphere both Romantic drama and grand opera, closely interrelated, arose.

The era of grand opera was foreshadowed in 1828 with *La Muette de Portici (The Mute of Portici)* by Daniel François Esprit Auber (1782–1871). Instead of subordinating music to the exigencies of the text, this work subordinated everything to

The pyrotechnics of grand opera required the use of extensive machinery to produce startling stage effects.

The Jewess (1835) by Jacques Halévy was one of the earliest grand operas.

music — in this case, a rather superficial sort of music. The dramatic power so poignantly expressed by Rameau, Gluck, and Cherubini was reduced to a meaningless exterior effect; and *La Muette*, in itself a work that contains much good operatic music and is carried by real élan, opened the way to the grand operas which are for music what the bourgeois drama is for literature.

The German Romantics naturally rejected this spectacular music. Mendelssohn called the ballet of the nuns in *Robert the Devil* (1831) "a veritable scandal." Schumann wrote that "the world has rarely seen such a conglomeration of monstrosities," and spoke of Meyerbeer as a "circus man." Nonetheless, Meyerbeer's influence upon the course of opera was conspicuous. He was one of the ablest dramatists in the whole history of opera, and as far as orchestration and dramatic accompaniment are concerned, Berlioz and Wagner owe much more to Meyerbeer than they were willing to admit.

As time passed, and the quietude of German Romanticism gave way to the expansive mood of the industrial age, even the Germans gave up their opposition to grand opera; and the King of Prussia invited Meyerbeer to become general director of music in Berlin.

Every new operatic style in France was originated by a foreigner — for instance, Lully and Gluck — so it is not surprising that the real founder of the French grand opera was a German, Jacob Liebmann Beer.

Giacomo Meyerbeer, a German musician and entrepreneur, became the most eloquent proponent of French grand opera.

When he came to France, Beer added to his family name that of one of his benefactors, Meyer, and also Italianized his first name; he thus became the famous composer, Giacomo Meyerbeer (1791–1864). With excellent instinct Meyerbeer divined the possibilities of grand opera, and succeeded in conquering the French public at his first try. His plays were grand spectacles in which the most bizarre figures paraded to the accompaniment of cleverly calculated music. Processions, councils, princesses on horseback, cardinals, and heretics were exhibited against a background of shipwrecks, cannonades, and tumbling cathedrals, accompanied by choirs of demons and corteges of phantoms.

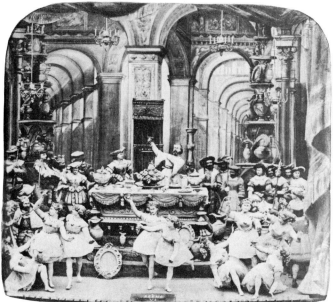

Ballet scene from Meyerbeer's The Prophet. *Early photograph.*

Eugène Scribe. French grand opera owed much to the dramatic skill of Scribe's librettos.

In THE MIDST of the general adulation of the operatic spectacular, from which the public obtained what it wanted, there appeared a curious figure, who was utterly misunderstood even by those who praised him to the skies. This was Gioacchino Rossini (1792–1868).

Rossini manifested Romantic tendencies in his early operas; then, in the *Barber of Seville* (1816), he harnessed his Romanticism to a Classical wit to give the world a work worthy of Beaumarchais and Mozart. Indeed, with his inexhaustible melodic gifts, his masterly characterizations, his uncanny knowledge of the stage, Rossini stands close to Mozart, and the *Barber* is a worthy companion to *Figaro*. None of Rossini's audiences could withstand the charms of his music, sparkling with spirit and caprice, overflowing with merriment, melodies, and rhythmic fireworks.

In *William Tell* (1829), the Italian composer demonstrated what he owed to French art and literature. The work is a mixture of music drama, *opera seria,* and grand opera: the old revolutionary opera lives in it, reinforced with pathos of the *opera seria* and the bombast of grand opera. Then, after the production of *William Tell,* something seemingly inexplicable happened. At the age of thirty-seven, when he had hardly reached the full development of his powers, Rossini ceased to compose operas.

120

The Italian Opera of
Rossini, Donizetti, and Bellini

During the remaining thirty-nine years of his life he produced nothing more for the stage, and nothing else of importance except the *Stabat Mater.*

Undoubtedly Rossini had seen the immense success of Meyerbeer's grand operas and realized that his own more graceful art was no longer possible. But two other operatic geniuses emerged from Italy who were able to overcome the superficial taste of the public. These composers were Gaetano Donizetti (1797–1848), and Vincenzo Bellini (1801–1835). Both were born to the

Gioacchino Rossini in his later years. After writing more than thirty operas in twelve years, he abruptly retired from composing for the stage at the age of 37

Gaetano Donizetti wrote more than sixty brilliantly melodious comic operas. In Lucia of Lammermoor *(1835), he proved himself to be a serious composer.*

Donizetti conducting a rehearsal for Don Pasquale *during his stay in Paris in 1843.*

Donizetti wrote his operas with great speed, often in a few days. A contemporary wit shows Donizetti composing with both hands.

operatic stage, both were imbued with the great traditions of Italian opera, and both realized that the principles of their national art were threatened by the new tastes emanating from Paris. Donizetti wrote one finished masterpiece, *Don Pasquale* (1843), a brilliant and consummate *opera buffa* in the best Italian tradition. Similarly, his earlier *Daughter of the Regiment* (1840), is a French *opéra comique* of eternal freshness, wit, and grace. Donizetti's facility and melodic inventiveness were beyond comprehension, satisfying both the public's appetite for melody and the singers' demand for virtuoso arias. There is a story that a bankrupt opera manager beseeched Donizetti for help; the composer set about to find a suitable subject, worked it into a libretto, composed the music, and prepared and conducted the production in nine days, and saved the manager's theater from its doom.

Bellini did not find the "eternal singing of arias" as tiresome as did the German and English critics, for when he sang he did not spare himself; everything sang in him, his whole soul bathed in the flowing melody, warm, caressing, and filled with desires, memories, passions. *La Sonnambula (The Sleepwalker),* and *Norma* (both 1831) are the works of a Romantic with a penchant for melancholy and softly elegiac melodies. *I Puritani (The Puritans;* 1835) shows how well Bellini approached the task of merging the styles of Italian and French opera. Bellini's early death prevented a lasting reconciliation between the two styles, and deprived opera of one of its great hopes.

Hector Berlioz in his mid-fifties when he was writing his grand opera, The Trojans. *A wit of the period described his head as "a large umbrella of hair projecting like a movable awning over the beak of a bird of prey."*

Hector Berlioz, Arch-Romantic

GRAND OPERA was the perfect expression of the insatiable urge for expansion that beset the Romantics in their desire to symbolize the intoxicating fullness and grandeur of life. Intensification, enhancement, and enlargement were native to them; they spoke of the poetry of poetry and of the philosophy of philosophy. The urge for the absolutist colossus, for the monumental, possessed the 19th century from the time of Napoleon and was manifest everywhere. The greatness worshipped by the age was not so much a static as a dynamic majesty — oppressive, powerful, and intolerant — and this force was embodied in one heaven-storming individual, Hector Berlioz (1803–1869).

With the champions of Romantic drama, Berlioz shared a preference for wild, demonic, and horrifying subjects and moods, a preference which demanded a pictorial and descriptive imagination. Indeed, the striving for literary expression and for the picturesque constitutes the most characteristic trait of French musical genius of all ages; and this French taste also helped to drive Berlioz to compose symphonic music that followed a clearly-defined literary program. At the same time the Romantic urge for the universal induced him to convert the symphony into a "drama without voices," and to attempt a symphonic form embracing poetry, music, and drama.

Berlioz sincerely believed that the roots of his art lay in Beethoven's symphonies, and that he was continuing the symphonic ideal which he interpreted as the embodiment of a poetic idea in music. He believed he could achieve this ideal through program music, and he did not understand that as a genre the symphony responds to

Young Hector Berlioz playing the guitar, an instrument on which he attained great virtuosity. He used the guitar and flute to teach himself the elements of music.

an abstract musical idea only. For this reason Berlioz's symphonies are a tragic conflict between mind and instinct. He succeeded in those movements which were free symphonic poems or scenes. When his fiery imagination could be given free rein, when he was setting a mood rather than endeavoring to depict a precise action, he composed music of the greatest originality and compelling genius. Berlioz himself eventually realized that the symphonic drama was not feasible. His quest for the unattainable Romantic ideal had to be continued, however, and in *The Damnation of Faust* he sought to "extract the musical essence from Goethe's *Faust*." This dramatic legend, midway between dramatic symphony and the music drama proper, is replete with fascinating music. Significantly, the best pieces are again those which allow a freedom of fantasy and are only loosely connected with the "essence" of Goethe's play.

Berlioz's lack of understanding of matters spiritual, his incapacity for meditation, made him the antithesis of a church composer. In his *Memoirs,* Berlioz said of the *Tuba Mirum* of his Requiem (which uses five orchestras) that its "grandeur was so terrible" that one of the choristers had a nervous collapse during the performance. Contemporary critics, perhaps impressed more by the size of the apparatus than the content of the work, called it a "triumphant success," and modern eulogists marvel at the virtuoso orchestral technique displayed in this score; but no one ever seems to associate this gigantic work with prayer for the departed souls.

At the end of his artistic career, this man of volcanic personality and fierce imagination looked back with profound discontent at the sum total of his efforts, seeing everywhere unfulfilled promises and unattained goals. His wealth of inspiration, the seriousness and strength of his artistic conviction, are impressive and manifest despite the uneven quality and the rigidity, at times even flatness, behind the great gestures; but there is not one finished work in his musical legacy.

Titlepage of the score of Berlioz's Damnation of Faust. *When Goethe's* Faust *appeared in a French translation, Berlioz, always susceptible to literary stimuli, set about conveying its essence into music.*

Berlioz conducting his giant orchestra. His contemporaries ridiculed his unconventional orchestration, and suggested that he employ a cannon in his performances.

Berlioz was closely connected throughout his career with the Concerts du Conservatoire. Established in 1828 this concert organization pioneered in the performance of many Romantic compositions.

Berlioz endeavored to bring everything, including opera, into the symphony: Franz Liszt (1811–1886) dreamed of a new type of music, "humanistic music," which would unite the dramatic element of the theater, the lyricism of symphony, and the devotional element of the church.

Only by a circuitous route did Liszt arrive at this avowed aim. Until about 1840 his compositions were almost exclusively piano pieces and transcriptions. After that date his interest shifted to vocal music, and the number of piano compositions dropped abruptly. Eventually his work centered around the orchestra and he abandoned composing for the piano almost completely, although he still retained his liking for vocal writing.

In the first period Liszt was attracted by the infinite tonal possibilities of the perfected piano; he sensed that immediateness of communication was possible to the pianist, and that the piano was able to compete with the orchestra. Romantic composers could express within the seven octaves of the piano keyboard ideas that had previously called for the use of several instruments; and consequently Schumann, Chopin, and the young Liszt preferred composing for the piano to any other medium.

Aware that the accepted orchestral language had reached both its apex and conclusion with Beethoven, Liszt consciously kept aloof from orchestral ventures. He recognized the identity of the Classical musical language with orchestral dialectics, and like the other Romantic composers, admired it; but he found Classical forms too confining for his Romantic desire for expansiveness. However, Liszt found a way out of this stylistic impasse. He saw clearly that even Chopin's admirably original method of composition would not suffice for the foundation of a new style; any new style would have to break completely with the past and reflect different aesthetic principles. His great achievement consisted in proving by his creation of the symphonic tone poem that it was possible to create a well-rounded and logically organized piece of music without forcing the ideas into the established frames of traditional forms.

Franz Liszt, Virtuoso and Symphonic Innovator

Franz Liszt playing before his friends in the house of Rossini in Rome. Sitting beside Liszt, leaning on the piano, is the Countess d'Agoult; seated behind him, George Sand and Alexandre Dumas, père; standing in the rear are Victor Hugo, Paganini, and Rossini. A bust of Beethoven is on the piano.

A cartoon of Liszt as a piano-winged hero destroying the dominance of rigid musical forms.

Liszt's orchestral compositions are generally based on a terse and seemingly simple figure or motif. The motif is elaborated to the point where even the accompanying figures are developed out of it — an eminently symphonic conception. Individual melodies derived from the basic motif are handled sometimes in a similar manner, sometimes in a contrasting fashion; and sometimes all of them are brought together in a kind of apotheosis at the end. Liszt used this method of composing so consistently that one must see in it a new principle of form — free form. Liszt broke completely with the Classical precepts of formal construction, thereby accomplishing what Ber-

lioz had wanted to do but had failed to realize.

Of Liszt's fourteen symphonic works, the *Faust Symphony*, consisting of three "character pictures," is the most outstanding by virtue of its wealth of ideas and their remarkable elaboration. Although this music is suggested and outlined on the basis of a literary inspiration, it is governed by purely musical factors, and this is its secret, the secret of true program music.

Franz Liszt occupies a unique position in the history of modern music; most of our accomplishments in the field of harmony, orchestration, and construction originated in his inquisitive and inspired mind. His will-

From 1840 to 1848, at the height of his power as a pianist, Liszt toured Europe triumphantly. Women in his audience swooned and fought for his belongings.

128

Liszt during his first stay in Weimar, when he served as the musical director of the Grand Ducal orchestra and opera (1848–1858).

ingness to support magnanimously every worthy undertaking even if his artistic preferences did not correspond with those of his protégés, his dazzling life as a virtuoso, his romantic love stories, his religious inclination, his brilliant literary essays, all created a compound personality which make it difficult to form a clear picture of both the man and the artist.

It was the tragedy of his life that he could never set aside his obligations as a virtuoso, an extraordinary pianist who had the public of the civilized world at his feet. The eclectic nature of his melodies, influenced by much travel, the rhetoric of the virtuoso, and the duties of a hard-pressed patron, pianist, composer, conductor, teacher, philosopher, conservatory president, and priest prevented his art from achieving maturity in the peace that it required. Liszt's extraordinary ability to draw a situation or a character with a few strokes often fascinates us even in the weakest passages; warmth of expression and the innately musical qualities of his invention seldom failed him. He may become noisy, bombastic, almost vulgar, but he always remains essentially musical.

Liszt in later years, after he had abandoned his career as a virtuoso and turned to teaching and conducting.

A choral festival at Budapest under the directorship of Liszt. In this city he helped to found the Hungarian Music Academy, and became its first president in 1874.

Richard Wagner. Never has there been a musician whose music so vitally affected the life and art of other generations.

Richard Wagner:
Creator of the Universal Art Work

"AT THE PRESENT TIME there are only three of us who belong together because we are alike." The three musicians alluded to in this quotation were Liszt, Berlioz, and the writer of the letter in which it appears, Richard Wagner (1813–1883). All three men wished to escape a pseudo-Classical idiom in order to avoid artistic servility, and all three were in quest of the unattainable Romantic ideal, the universal, all-embracing work of art.

This concept of an all-embracing artwork, especially as Wagner thought of it, was not merely an aesthetic ideal. It was a philosophical precept capable of freeing modern man. Wagner felt that life in his society was opposed to the creative mission of man; that it was passive, lacking in will, and therefore inhuman. He felt that although man's destiny was to be life's master, man was gradually becoming life's servant, and that the divergence between action and thought was bringing mankind to its doom. Wagner resolved to lead men back to a unity of action and thought, body and soul — the kind of creative activity which does not separate any problems from life.

Like Nietzsche, Wagner felt that mankind was in need of a new mythology. Therefore, he went back to the creative force inherent in the ancient Germanic myth, and repopulated Valhalla, the dwelling place of the German gods and heroes. He placed art once more at the center of a religious cult which glorified pure, heroic, divine action.

Although Wagner's music is rooted in Romanticism, this proponent of an operatic superart to replace religion refused to listen to Romanticism's celestial whispers. Superlatives were the real fare of this man and success a matter of course. Such forceful, purposeful, dynamic, sensuous, and premeditated ideals are in contradiction to the longing for the endless, the ethereal, and the disembodied which motivated the Romantics. In his art the blue flower of the Romantics wilts in the heat of passion, and longing for the infinite gives way to the will for power.

Wagner himself wanted to be more than a great musician. He felt that the new music he created was merely the path to the complete reorganization of life in his own spirit, a spirit which desired that the world be dominated by German culture; and indeed Wagner contributed as much, if not more, to the rising superiority complex of the Second Reich as Bismarck. Nothing illustrates this more appropriately than the well-known picture of Emperor William II standing with his Lohengrin helmet before a swan — the Knight of the Grail of German imperialism.

Considered separately, Wagner's drama and poetry are weak, his characterizations often mere rhetoric, his music sometimes great, sometimes merely labored; but considered as a whole, he is formidable and unique. His artistic language is a theatrical language, it does not suffer a small place. It was the voice of a people, the voice of a Germany which wanted to be heard in all four corners of the world; and it was heard, and it was heeded.

The first performance of Rienzi *was given in Dresden in 1842, and was so successful that Wagner was made conductor of the opera house.*

WAGNER'S ROMANTIC OPERAS

No man or artist can be separated from his predecessors, and Wagner too began his creative work under the influence of the reigning musical forces. He started out with the old fairy opera, *Die Feen (The Fairies)*, whence he progressed to historic grand opera *(Rienzi)*, and then to romantic opera *(The Flying Dutchman)* in the wake of Weber and Marschner, reaching its height in *Tannhäuser* and *Lohengrin*.

At this point, a sharp stylistic and ideological change occurred in Wagner's

work. The revolutionary year of 1849 gave us the Wagner who altered the course of history. Exiled from the social and human community of German art for his political activity, he became free of its conventions, was able to stand outside the artistic world, and no longer had to partake in its development. His enormous strength manifested itself in the fact that he did not try to regain his lost connections, but instead set out to create a world of his own in which his art could grow unmolested. Uniting in himself all the restraining weaknesses of his century, Wagner developed them actively into Promethean works of tremendous intensity: the highest pathos of passion, the darkest pessimism, uncontrollable sensuous fervor, and a tormented desire for fulfillment and redemption.

The technical and spiritual foundation of the "universal work of art" was a new unity between music and drama based on the forms of old German alliterative poetry, the *Stabreim*, and on fundamental musical themes, *leitmotives*, which acted as recurring motives of reminiscence. The leitmotif principle was not new; what Wagner did was to employ it as an integral, dominating stylistic-constructive factor. The constant manipulation of predetermined thematic material inevitably leads to a symphonic technique. Consequently, in Wagner's operas the point of gravity passed from the voices to the orchestra, which was not bound by the technical and aesthetic limitations of the voice and responded with ease to abstract musical requirements.

Wagner gradually added to the wonderfully expressive symphonic idiom of the Classic and early Romantic eras an infinitely more flexible and modernized orchestral technique, of which he still remains the unsurpassed master. *Rienzi, The Flying Dutchman, Tannhäuser,* and *Lohengrin,* all written between 1842 and 1850, still have the structure of the conventional romantic opera with arias, recitatives, duets, and choruses treated as independent units. In the operas written after 1850, the orchestra becomes dominant and the singers, although still taking part in the tremendous tonal drama, are at times helpless, entirely carried by the symphonic torrent.

Wagner during his stay in Dresden, in the 1840's.

Tannhäuser: *Wagner succeeded in this opera in creating a dramatic atmosphere that gains in intensity up to the end.*

Lohengrin *represents the culmination of German Romantic opera, and marks the turning point in Wagner's life. It made him an important figure on the musical scene.*

The Flying Dutchman: *as no other work, this opera conjures up the atmosphere of the sea. The score echoes Wagner's experiences during a flight from Riga in 1849 to escape his creditors.*

The Rhinegold

The Valkyrie

THE RING OF THE NIBELUNGS

Tʜᴇ ᴡʀɪᴛɪɴɢ of the four dramas comprising the *Ring* progressed in a curious manner. First came the last one, *The Twilight of the Gods;* then, finding this gigantic piece too summary, Wagner prefaced it with *Siegfried*, which in turn needed additional preparation, which *The Valkyrie* furnished. Then all three were introduced by *The Rhinegold.* The peculiar growth of the dramatic story of the *Ring* doomed its unity from the outset; Wagner could not master it dramatically, and it is a sheer wonder that the musician was able to triumph over the long and rambling repetitions by the power of his symphonic eloquence.

Siegfried

Twilight of the Gods

Wagner's preoccupation with Schopenhauer's philosophy and his love for Mathilde Wesendonk led him to put aside the quarreling Germanic gods and heroes; and under the impulse of his great passion he composed his most powerful, most romantic, and most fervent drama, *Tristan and Isolde.* Completed in 1859 the opera carries the sensuous expressiveness of music to its ultimate limits. The orchestra moves in incessant modulations, in a sea of constantly wavering tonality, which mirrors an adequate portrayal of the restlessly glowing passions that fire the drama.

Wagner followed *Tristan* with a real play, *Die Meistersinger von Nürnberg (The Master Singers of Nuremberg).* In *Die Meistersinger* the blood-boiling chromaticism of *Tristan,* with its shifting, dark tonalities, disappears before a sturdy diatonic idiom and a radiating C-major sunshine. The German musical past is reborn in the opera in chorale, fugue, basso ostinato, German song, lute music, and cantus firmus motet; the old operatic devices of ensembles, processionals, and dances are again admitted to their rightful place and the result is a spectacle that warms one's heart.

To continue composing with the unperformed scores of *The Rhinegold, The Valkyrie, Tristan,* and *Meistersinger* buried in the drawers of his desk required a degree of artistic integrity against which all of Wagner's insincere acts pale to insignificance. But with all his determination, his situation was desperate until a royal patron changed all this into a sudden Canaan. Ludwig II of Bavaria, like a youthful fairy-tale prince, rescued the distressed composer and placed his kingdom at Wagner's disposal. Their friendship reached its climax with the building of a theater at Bayreuth for the genius of Germandom. In 1876 the theater opened with three complete performances of the *Ring,* and Wagner's lifelong dream came to fulfillment.

Tristan and Isolde

Die Meistersinger

135

Ludwig II. He became King of Bavaria at nineteen. Wagner's music was the passion of his life, and he was anxious to use his power to serve the composer. He saved Wagner from debtor's prison in 1864, and without Ludwig's patronage, Bayreuth would never have become a reality.

BAYREUTH AND *PARSIFAL*

The beginning of the Bayreuth Festival House: On May 22, 1872, Wagner's fifty-ninth birthday, the cornerstone was laid to the strains of his own Imperial March.

After BAYREUTH had been founded, the master, imperious and unrelenting as ever, summoned his powers for a final effort. He intended to create something to crown his lifework which would at the same time be beyond the reach of ordinary controversy or criticism because of its subject matter. The result was *Parsifal*.

Wagner's known lack of religious feelings and his generally insincere nature suggest he had motives other than religious when he wrote this consecrational festival play. Indeed, *Parsifal* was a super-romantic opera, a theatrical fairy drama designed for the edification of the sanctimonious bourgeois of the new German Reich. To express its credo Wagner drew material from legends and sagas and made his heroes into symbols, abstract types, rather than into creatures of reality. At the height of passion it becomes irrelevant what these figures say, for they are merely pawns without identity, they dissolve in pure music. With its excessive length and interminable soliloquies *Parsifal* can be very trying; yet at times the music becomes eloquent beyond anything Wagner had written before.

Parsifal, *Wagner's last great triumph. After its first performance in 1882, it had to be repeated sixteen times.*

Tea at Villa Wahnfried in Bayreuth; from left to right: Richard Wagner, Cosima Wagner (daughter of Liszt), the artist Jablonski, Paul Zhukowsky (designer of the sets for Parsifal).

Germany's leading orchestra, the Gewandhaus Orchestra in Leipzig about 1840, a modest assemblage of players.

The Wagnerian orchestra of Bayreuth (1882). Note the large number of string and brass players as compared to the Gewandhaus Orchestra. The orchestra pit at Bay-reuth was enclosed to effect a sonorous blend of all the sections. Wagner is at the top, prompting conductor Herman Levi through the opening during a rehearsal.

138

The ophicleide was widely used in the Paris orchestras of Berlioz's time.

Adolph Saxe and his sax horn which became an important orchestral element.

Enrichment of the Orchestra

THE BEGINNING OF THE Romantic era, and the advent of program music and grand opera all contributed to a considerable enlargement of the orchestra. In Mendelssohn's time, about 1840, the Leipzig Gewandhaus Orchestra, one of the few independent concert orchestras (most of the others were opera orchestras which also gave concerts), consisted of about sixteen to twenty violins, five violas, four cellos, four basses, and the usual complement of winds. This was the norm; but in the big opera houses — Covent Garden, Milan, Munich, Paris, or Naples — the strings were fifty or sixty strong.

Furthermore, the orchestra increased in size as new instruments were added. The English horn, bass clarinet, trombones, a second pair of horns, harp, all manner of percussion instruments joined the ensemble; this necessitated enlarging the string body. Besides growing larger, the orchestra also became more mobile with the introduction of the valve mechanism which permitted horns and trumpets to play all the notes in the chromatic scale. With Wagner, the tubas, contrabass, trombone, bass trumpet, a second harp part, and other newcomers appear; the number of woodwinds was raised from pairs to a group of three (later four); and the horns increased from four to eight.

Vuillaume's twelve-foot octobass, pitched one octave below the cello.

139

Jullien, a true showman-conductor, staged large concerts in London. He conducted Beethoven with a special baton.

Three Bayreuth conductors: left to right, Herman Levi, Hans Richter, and Felix Mottl.

Emergence of the Virtuoso Conductor

François Habeneck was one of the first modern conductors of symphonic music. Originally a violinist, he remained a violin-bow conductor.

Hans von Bülow. He made the German orchestra a model for the orchestras of all other countries.

Liszt was the first conductor to use body movements and facial expressions to convey essential phrasing, rhythm, and dynamics to the orchestra.

Wagner was phenomenal even as a conductor. His book On Conducting *(1869) shows he was thoroughly familiar with the practices of both the old and new schools.*

CONDUCTING IS a very old musical practice whose origins are lost in history; but the art as we know it, that is, leadership by an individual who is not a member of the performing group itself, dates from about 1800. The conductor was replacing the old "master at the keyboard" and the bow-wielding concertmaster. By the end of the second decade of the 19th century, Weber and Spohr were conducting with a white birch baton, although not without opposition from the old guard. Weber was the first outstanding conductor in the modern sense; he bestowed the same conscientious care on the works of his colleagues as he did on his own. So did Mendelssohn. Otto Nicolai (1810–1849), who founded the Vienna Philharmonic, was their counterpart in the south. Berlioz, a very able conductor, was the first guest conductor. But perhaps the greatest, most feared, and most admired conductor before Wagner was Gasparo Spontini (1774–1851), who ruled Berlin with an iron hand. Then came the famous Wagner conductors, developed by the master: Hans von Bülow, Hans Richter, Hermann Levi, and of course, even before them, Liszt.

Anton Bruckner

ALTHOUGH THE REVERBERATIONS of Wagner's ideas were felt in every field of music, few composers openly admitted their indebtedness to him. One of these few was Anton Bruckner (1824–1896) who, despite his Wagnerian credo, stands rather outside his time. He lived in a small-town clerical atmosphere; but he reveled in the pomp of Wagner's orchestra, and the boldness of Beethoven; and his Masses and symphonies combine a childlike medieval religiosity with the verbosity of the post-Romantic idiom.

This medieval soul living in the 19th century struggled with the problem of finding an artistic relationship to God. He dedicated a symphony "to the good Lord," and found an adequate and congenial expression for his mystic soul in his Masses, which with Liszt's similar works are undoubtedly the most significant Catholic church music written in the Romantic and post-Romantic eras.

Bruckner's symphonies from the first epic utterances are torrents of music, great hymns, broad and inundating; they therefore offend against the essence of symphonic thought, which is logic and economy. Bruckner is a perpetual eulogizer, always the same, always saying the same thing in the same way, with the sameness of a majestic river. Some of his symphonies have no individuality, no particular mood; indeed, his whole symphonic output is one large poem. Like Brahms, Bruckner attempted to cleanse music of the extramusical literary components forced on the art by Romanticism; but by the time he wrote, the symphony was no longer a living force. What Brahms could achieve with the utmost discipline of thought, Bruckner could match only in certain details — a beautiful slow movement, a bold scherzo, a dreamy Romantic exposition. Not one of his works attains true symphonic greatness.

Anton Bruckner in his Vienna apartment. He fought a tragic struggle for recognition. Originally an organist, his symphonies are gigantic organ fantasies.

Book Five

Max Klinger: Brahms Fantasies

THE TWILIGHT
OF ROMANTICISM

Johannes Brahms. His friend von Bülow ranked his music with that of Bach and Bee-thoven. Brahms thought of himself modestly as a searcher and a craftsman. Basically a shy man, he hated publicity and even refused to have his portrait painted.

144

Johannes Brahms

ALTHOUGH BERLIOZ, Liszt, and Wagner had the center of the stage in the period of waning Romanticism they were not the only composers of great music. For at this time, three artists appeared who must be ranked with the greatest composers of the world: Brahms, Bizet, and Verdi. Vastly different in their aim and backgrounds, these three had something in common: they were opposed not so much to the prevailing musical style as to the literary and philosophical orientation of the music of Berlioz and Wagner; they wanted to restore music to its own kingdom.

Johannes Brahms (1833–1897) was a musician who tried to be as universal as Beethoven, who was equally at home in all domains of music except opera, and who knew what the majestic symphony, the ample oratorio, and the all-but-forgotten organ demanded as their true and rightful patrimony. Of all the composers writing after the death of Schubert, Brahms was the only one who approached the Beethovenian ideal, and no one else was able to reconstruct true symphonic thought as he did; but that one word, *reconstruct*, qualifies his whole art.

Brahms could not achieve the impossible: he could not altogether recapture the serenity of the Classicist. Hence the note of resignation that envelops his works, the pessimism which is his outlook on life. His illness was the Romantic illness; he had to try to combat the overflowing richness of the Romantic soul with discipline, and to limit, bind, and balance it with art and study.

A great admirer of Schumann, Brahms began his career with compositions for the pianoforte; but among these are three sonatas. The use of the sonata form was most unusual for a Romantic, especially a young one, for the reigning type was the "moment musical," the small lyric form. These youthful piano compositions spurn the wonderfully developed Romantic piano style. They have a peculiar pianism of their own, and the great conflict, the struggle against Beethoven's shadow, that accompanied Brahms throughout his life is evident here, at the beginning of his career. More than once one is conscious of a deepseated desire for symphonic expression which makes these works, as Schumann said, "veiled symphonies."

While Brahms took to the composition of piano music and mixed chamber music with relative ease, his approach to the two greatest forms of the Classic era, the string quartet and symphony, was most cautious and time-consuming. This fact is of great importance in judging Brahms. For in reality he was a Romantic, and, like Schumann, instinctively drawn to the smaller, intimate forms. What drove him toward the large forms was a longing for, an invincible attraction to, the great art of the German past — and perhaps he also had a desire to save it.

Brahms's scholarly knowledge of certain phases of musical history was as thorough as any musicologist's of his time. It was this familiarity with the problems of the music of the past that made him hesitate at first to approach the large symphonic forms. The D minor Piano Concerto of 1859, for instance, was planned as a symphony; then, as the composer felt his inability to sustain such a large symphonic structure, it was reduced to a sonata for two pianos. A few years later, the composition had assumed a pianistic complexion, but still showed its orchestral origins; and Brahms converted it into a piano concerto. The finale, which originally defeated the symphonic plan, was replaced by a rondo, but this still does not rise to the level of the first movements, and this noble and tragic work remains a unique hybrid, a symphony with obbligato piano.

In the first and last movements of Brahms's four symphonies, written between 1876 and 1885, the frame is often more extensive than originally conceived because the form is expanded in all directions by elaboration. In order to fill the immense spaces thus created, the content had to be enriched artificially. This is why those large movements are so "difficult to understand"; but it is also in these extensions that Brahms's great artistry, his grasp of polyphonic and variation technique, shows itself in all its power. And when his inspiration is left undisturbed both by his penchant for complications and by the willful interference of the learned connoisseur of the past, he reaches the highest peak that orchestral music had known since the death of Schubert. The Fourth Symphony, the greatest of the series, is the most melancholy and the most consciously archaic. Melancholy, seldom missing in Brahms's art, is here the dominating mood penetrating every fiber of the work. The culminating point of the symphony is the last movement, in which the composer leads us into the immense halls of Baroque music.

Brahms's creative life was planned with care and circumspection. The smaller choral works ended in the *Requiem*, the piano trios and quartets in the symphonies. After he finished his Second Symphony he progressed to the works of the late period, rich in experience and assuredness. But even so, he never lost sight of his august predeces-

sors, and whenever he embarked on a new venture he tried to find immediate connections with the past. In his violin sonatas Brahms began at the point where Beethoven's last G-major sonata had stopped, and wrote a work in the same key, following this with two more sonatas. Although he was able to restore the artistic unity of this genre, his sonatas sin as badly against euphony and clarity as any others written by the Romantics.

His piano parts are tremendously overloaded and swollen, and make it very difficult for the violin to be heard on an equal basis. This pianistic hypertrophy is less oppressive in other works written for piano-string ensemble, but the writing is particularly felicitous when Brahms uses wind instruments in his ensembles. The quintet for strings and clarinet is a composition of incomparable nobility of thought and sound.

Two lifelong friends of Johannes Brahms: Joseph Joachim, a famous Hungarian violinist, and Clara Schumann.

Brahms at twenty-three when he visited the Schumanns at Düsseldorf in
1853. Robert Schumann noted in his
diary, "Brahms to see me, a genius."

The medallion with their picture which the Schumanns
gave to young Brahms. He
kept it all his life.

After he had settled in Vienna in 1862,
Brahms's life was uneventful. He made
a few concert tours and took summer
trips to the Austrian lakes and Italy.

Brahms in his early thirties, when he was
writing the German Requiem. Its first
performance under the composer's direction took place in Bremen in 1868.

Brahms the pianist. His
touch was magic.

Brahms as a conductor
was self-possessed.

A silhouette of Brahms making his twice-daily trip to the Red Hedgehog, a meeting place for artists.

Although the song occupied a central position in Brahms's art, the genre remained as problematical to him as did the symphony. In the Romantic song of the 19th century, the instrumental part had gradually assumed a paramount importance. In contrast to this Romantic treatment, Brahms placed the singing voice in the foreground and did not permit the accompaniment any rights beyond its essentially subordinate role. Beginning with his first song, *Liebestreue*, Opus 3, a sad, pessimistic composition, unhappy love is the subject of the majority of his serious songs. He was markedly partisan to the strophic form, and set some children's songs and folksongs which, in their simplicity and heartfelt sincerity, belong among the greatest examples of this art.

In the second half of the 19th century, the choral song, formerly a secondary field for the great Romantic musicians, found in Brahms a composer who dedicated himself to it with the same earnestness that characterized his great works. His choral works culminate in the *German Requiem*, which will remain his most beloved work, a Protestant Office for the Dead such as German music had not known since the days of its great Biblical composers of the Baroque era. Unlike the Latin Requiem Mass which prepares the souls for the *Dies Irae*, this *German Requiem* comforts the bereaved; utter peace envelops the whole work, and only once, in the terrifying unison passages of the mysterious funeral march, are we reminded of the tragedy of death.

Brahms was the Lord Keeper of the Seal of the Classic heritage, the composer in whom all the Classic ideals were united once more before they were finally lost in chaos. In him Classicism became merely a beautiful gesture, whereas in Beethoven it was fulfillment and synthesis. It was Brahms's tragedy that Beethoven's shadow followed him everywhere.

148

Brahms accompanying a performance of his songs by Alice Barbi at the Bösendorfer Concert Hall of Vienna.

Brahms with Johann Strauss at Ischl, an Austrian spa. Brahms was fond of Strauss waltzes, and composed some waltzes himself.

Eduard Hanslick, a Viennese critic, offers his adulation to Brahms, whom many considered the exponent of an anti-Wagner bloc.

Georges Bizet in 1860, when he returned from his Italian journey as winner of the Prix de Rome.

CARMEN
Opera-Comique en quatre actes

MEILHAC et L. HALÉVY   MUSIQUE de GEORGES BIZET

Poster for first run of Carmen *at the Opéra Comique. Bizet wrote this opera of Spanish life without ever having visited Spain.*

Henri Meilhac and Ludovic Halévy transformed Mérimée's story of Carmen *into a libretto of great dramatic power.*

Georges Bizet and Carmen

TOWARD THE MIDDLE of the 19th century the fire and expansive power of French Romanticism subsided. The public's taste tired of uncritical flights of imagination and of eternal stories whose complicated artificiality belied reality; audiences began to demand a new orientation more in conformity with the phenomena of life. Thus Naturalism arose as a direct opposition, a conscious reaction, to Romanticism. Its adherents wanted to paint human beings and human aspiration with faithful accuracy.

This current of Naturalism brought to the fore one of the most dramatic operas in the history of the lyric stage, a work that towers above all plays and operas of the period: *Carmen*, with a text by Meilhac and Halévy and music by Georges Bizet (1838–1875). *Carmen* represented a totally new orientation in opera. Its subject was taken from a short story by Prosper·Mérimée; the libretto preserves the original savage and lifelike beauty of Mérimée's work. It is an opera of unique impact; its lyrical parts disseminate a tender and suave melancholy in which nothing is stylized, and the work as a whole has an almost brutal force.

149

Pauline Lucca created the role of Carmen on the German operatic stage.

Céléstine Galli-Marié, the first Carmen, gave a realistic performance which emphasized the story's seamier aspects.

Emma Calvé, considered the greatest Carmen.

Bizet's Pearl Fishers, produced in 1863, had only a limited run.

Carmen was at first rejected by the French public and the musical world. Those very people who admired the realistic and naturalistic novel and drama rejected the same elements in this music drama, which for sheer power and plausibility towered above anything which that generation produced.

This drama, swift and undisguised in its music, with its overheated southern temperament, dazzling and vital orchestra, wonderful harmonies, inescapable melodies, called forth the enthusiastic homage of Nietzsche, who saw in Carmen the eternal model of the lyric drama, a conclusion which was also an indictment of Wagnerian operatic aesthetics.

Bizet was equally unfortunate with his

early operas, The Pearl Fishers (1863) and The Fair Maiden of Perth (1867). He expected a definitive success from his incidental music to Daudet's L'Arlésienne, but its reception was icy and Daudet's friends worried lest the bad impression created by the music cast a shadow on the play itself. Today Daudet's play is chiefly remembered because of Bizet's music, music of such freshness, limpidity, and piquancy as the second half of the 19th century seldom heard. Curiously enough, the two orchestral suites made from the music to L'Arlésienne are classified as "light music," and are usually performed by park bands, pop orchestras, and other popular organizations; the august philharmonic societies play them only in their matinées for children.

Giuseppe Verdi: Composer and Patriot

THE AUSTRIAN RULE of Italy after the Napoleonic wars created a tremendous political reaction in that country, already seething with the patriotism and liberalism engendered earlier by the French Revolution. Italian nationalism received another powerful impetus from French Romanticism, for the Romantic cult of the past and of the exotic offered a great variety of subjects in which could be expressed the desires and aims of Italy's suffering patriots. These nationalistic sentiments are reflected in contemporary Italian opera: and in the works of one Italian opera composer, Giuseppe Verdi (1813–1901), we find the highest expression of Italian arts and letters contemporary with the Wagnerian era. The heroic tinge in Verdi's operas does not pale even though the political events that evoked them have been forgotten. His music is eternally human, bold, dramatic, full-bodied, and Italian in every detail.

Verdi wrote during a period of indecision in Italian opera. As in France, grand opera reigned supreme. The Italian facility of invention, blended with the showmanship of grand opera, produced the shallowest and most ephemeral of styles. It is the more remarkable that, after a few false starts, Verdi found his own way regardless of the models before and around him. *Nabucco* (1842), although still showing traces of the perilous influence of French-Italian conven-

tional opera, exhibits an energetic conduct of melody, a fresh rhythmic and metric articulation that were unknown among most composers of Verdi's generation.

Then, in the 1840's, the nationalistic movement, approaching revolutionary intensity, carried him away. This deeply religious patriot used subjects that in the face of a strictly enforced censorship nevertheless conveyed an allegorical meaning to his compatriots waiting for deliverance from the Austrian yoke: *Ernani* (1844), *Giovanna d'Arco* (1845), *Attila* (1846), and *I Masnadieri* (1847), made his name synonymous with the Italian cause; and when in his *Battaglia di Legnano (The Battle of Legnano;* 1848) the knights swore an oath to repulse Italy's tyrants from beyond the Alps, the public's frenzy knew no bounds. This period of Verdi's creative activity ended with *Luisa Miller* (1849), after which the now famous composer retired to a country estate in his home district.

Giuseppe Verdi holding the score of Nabucco (Nebuchadnezzar), *the opera which started him on his rise to fame.*

"Viva Verdi" was a popular war cry throughout Italy, for the Italians associated the letters of the composer's name with the initials of the patriotic slogan Vittorio Emmanuele Re d'Italia.

151

The quartet from the third act of Rigoletto, *a high point of operatic writing.*

Marie Duplessis, a courtesan, was the prototype of Violetta in La Traviata.

La Traviata *was Verdi's adaptation of Dumas' play. Its première in 1853 was "an out-and-out fiasco."*

In the 1850's, Verdi, the provincial landowner, who spent his free time reading Shakespeare, Schiller, and the Greek dramatists, surprised the world by writing *Rigoletto* (1851), *Il Trovatore (The Troubadours)* (1853), and *La Traviata (The Lost One)* (1853), three of the most universally known operas in the history of the lyric stage. None of the grand operas ever attained the sincere and profound pathos, the lyricism, and the virile artistic conviction that issue from these works. And they have much more: a masterly arrangement of motives and a grasp of harmonic and tonal relationship which made Verdi the true and worthy successor of the great Classic opera composers and a formidable rival of Richard Wagner.

The Verdi of the 1870's was no longer satisfied with merely giving every character his dramatic tone: he wanted to delineate the dramatic *task* of each character. Therefore he began to draw away from grand opera. His new style appears in *Aïda* (1871); this opera is more lavish in pomp and fanfare than the most spectacular grand opera, but its dazzling exterior is only one aspect of a grandiose conception of drama in which passionate accents and delicate genre scenes represent the two poles between which the drama takes its course.

Verdi conducts a performance of Aïda *in Paris.*

152

The Masked Ball *was scheduled in 1858 to open in Naples, but the opera's story was too inflammatory for the censors. Verdi refused to make any changes, and his stand made him a national hero.*

Il Trovatore, *first performed in 1853, had been written in twenty-eight days.*

In Aïda *Verdi created an opera more lavish in pomp and fanfare than the most spectacular grand opera. Arias, pageants, and scenes of jealousy and love are skillfully combined.*

153

Verdi playing for Arrigo Boito. In 1879, the composer renewed his acquaintance with Boito, a gifted writer and musician, who wrote the librettos for Otello *and* Falstaff.

After a long interlude in which Verdi produced only the *Requiem Mass* (1874), the seventy-three-year-old composer broke his silence with *Otello* (1887), a work which bears the stamp of genius at its pinnacle from its opening "storm chorus," a scene of elemental power, to the indescribably sad last song of Desdemona and the tragic end of Othello. After *Otello* Verdi could not rest. Returning to a field he had not cultivated for some forty years, at the age of almost eighty he began where Mozart and Rossini had left off in their thirties to write an *opera buffa. Falstaff* (1892) is, indeed, an *opera buffa*, but the laughter in it is not mere harmless merriment but the laughter of wisdom, the amusement of a great and experienced connoisseur of life who had lived through generations and learned their changing ways.

Verdi was harshly misjudged by the contemporary critics, who said he wrote Italian operas with hurdy-gurdy melodies and guitarlike orchestral accompaniments. Many critics resented his refusal to become a satellite of Wagner; but Verdi's method and approach were fundamentally different from the ponderous, metaphysical, problem-seek-

Verdi conducting the Requiem Mass *composed at the death of Alessandro Manzoni (1785–1873), an Italian patriot and novelist.*

ing spirit of the master of Bayreuth. Verdi raised no fundamental issues of world outlook; man and his fate remained his subject, and all problems were solved with innate musicianship and Latin grace.

Man and artist were singularly united and complemented in Verdi, and it is well-nigh impossible to understand one without knowing the other. What a difference between the insincere and domineering Wagner, always craving publicity and issuing manifestos to his friends, and the retiring, severely upright, and incorruptible Italian maestro, who refused a small fortune rather than make minor changes in one of his librettos.

The ruler of a little empire, employed some two hundred workers on his estate, and looked after the wellbeing of his charges with the benevolence of a father. When times were hard he raised their wages, and the not inconsiderable earnings of his model farm — he was a competent agriculturist — were invested in foundations to help needy musicians. The great modesty which motivated his philanthropic acts was equaled by the artist's calm and absolutely sincere conviction of the nature and place of his art in the world of music. Yet all he said after the most overwhelming successes was *"Il tempo deciderà"* — "Time will decide."

Victor Maurel as Falstaff. In 1892 Verdi had one of his greatest triumphs in Falstaff, *adapted by Boito from Shakespeare's* Merry Wives *and* Henry IV.

Verdi and Victor Maurel after the première of Otello *in 1887. Written when Verdi was seventy-three, this opera shows Verdi still powerfully inventive.*

A sketch of Verdi in his old age, by Boldini.

155

Edouard de Reszke, a member of the Paris Opera, who sang Mephistopheles in the New York performances of Faust.

French Opera: Bourgeois and Opulent

Charles Gounod trying his hand at painting in the studio of his friend Ingres.

The staircase of the Paris Opera, a symbol of the bourgeoisie's taste for opulence and ostentation.

FRANCE, in the second half of the 19th century, was not blessed with the appearance of so great a musician and so great a man as Verdi. The French composers of the end of the century gave the public what it wanted, and what it wanted was mainly opera. No one paid attention to anything else but the lyric stage, traditionally the national genre of France. This age of triumphant capitalism had brought the indefatigable, prudent French citizen to a degree of wellbeing that made him anxious to indulge his yearning for art — by which he meant caressing melodies, and pleasant stories and plots which would make him forget the worries of daily existence.

Consequently, dramatic tirades, the harsh cries of passion, and the sorrowful accents of tragedy and suffering gave way to pleasing couplets and amorous cantilenas. Jules Massenet (1842–1912) and his *Manon,* Charles Gounod (1818–1893) and his *Romeo and Juliet* and Ambroise Thomas (1811–1896) and his *Mignon* came on the scene.

After many unsuccessful tries, Charles Gounod had his only lasting world success with the operatic setting of the Margaret episode from Faust. In this *Marguerite,* or as it was later somewhat exaggeratedly rechristened, *Faust* (1859), Gounod returned to the day before yesterday, to Boieldieu's refined, ironical, and skeptical gracefulness. Gounod was more naïve than his predecessor; on the other hand, his musicianship was more instinctive and his melodic gifts more substantial. In the song-like numbers of *Faust* one can hear the traditional dance rhythms of the French lyric stage. This rediscovery of tradition gave strength to Gounod and to the trend he represents; step by step he displaced Meyerbeer's grand opera which by then appeared grandiloquent and pompous. One should not look for great literary ambitions in Gounod's work, however. *Faust* and *Romeo and Juliet* have no kinship with Goethe and Shakespeare; they are too sweet and perfumed.

Charles Gounod conducting. His Faust *was enormously popular.*

Ambroise Thomas as a young man. His opera Mignon *had an unprecedented success.*

The orchestra of the Paris Opera, as painted by Edgar Degas. French composers added glamour to their operas by including ballets.

157

Jules Massenet in his Paris home. The plushy elegance displayed suggests a comparison with the general character of Massenet's music.

A cartoon of Saint-Saëns drawn by his fellow musician, Gabriel Fauré. His intelligence and eclecticism made Saint-Saëns a great power in French music.

Jules Massenet was essentially an imitator in whose numerous works one can follow the history of opera in the second half of the century — that is, the history of successful operas — the difference being only that in his hands operatic ideas were emasculated and sentimentalized. Still, Massenet had an extensive knowledge of the theater, and his facile melodic gift should not be minimized. He was the poet of beautiful sinners and their loves. *Manon* is the outstanding example of his work — a competent, clever, and scented mixture of little character and much sentimentality, which well captured the spirit of Abbé Prévost's novel.

Camille Saint-Saëns (1835—1921), another prominent figure of this period, is the perfect example of the eclectic musician of talent. His musical gifts matured on the study of the classics, but nothing in the new musical movements escaped his attention; he knew everything and used everything. Active in all branches of music, he was equally at home in all of them, for his positive, intelligent, reasoning, and precise mind always advised the creative musician in him. Nonetheless, his clever music lacks conviction and ardor, and today sounds faded.

Camille Saint-Saëns's opera, Samson and Delilah, *fulfilled the desires of a prosperous bourgeoisie for a spectacular show. It has a melodious fluency, but lacks the accents of genuine passion.*

Characters from

Orpheus in Hades.

Offenbach in his Paris studio, where he turned out operettas at a frantic pace. He confessed, "I shall die with a melody at the end of my pen."

The Sprightly World of Offenbach and Strauss

Despite the taste for the saccharine works of Massenet and his school, there was enough Gallic wit and spirit left in the people of Paris to enjoy a hearty laugh at their own folly. And once again it was a foreigner who exerted a fresh influence on the French lyric stage.

Born a German, Jacques Offenbach (1819–1880) went to Paris at an early age. After some study at the Paris Conservatory, he became a member of the orchestra of the Opéra Comique, and afterward a conductor of his own works in different theaters. His music is characterized by a radiant fresh spirit, elegance, and a light ironic tone. He can be frivolous, biting, and arrogant, but also genuinely moving. The adventurous and flirtatious elements in his works seem somewhat cynical, but this great expert of the human marionette theater that was the Second Empire felt that his contemporaries were too small to inspire tragic greatness. He ridiculed the frivolous and lighthearted life of Napoleon III's Paris with biting sarcasm and humor; but at the same time he enjoyed being part of it.

Offenbach approached his work with a musical equipment and technique which allowed him to produce the unsurpassed, even unequaled, model of the modern operetta. His small, finely-wrought forms, lilting or slightly lascivious dances, ingratiating and impudent melodies, remarkable declamation whittled to a fine point, rhythmic verve, and brilliant, piquant, yet supple orchestration have not lost an iota of their freshness. His works — *Orpheus in Hades, Parisian Life, The Fair Helen* — still have a genuine attraction, since they expose essential human truths and follies.

Character from La Périchole.

Jacques Offenbach. He started his career as a virtuoso cellist at the Opéra Comique after coming to Paris at fourteen.

Offenbach during his American tour in 1875. He undertook this trip to recoup money lost in his theatrical enterprises.

The Gods of Olympus dance the infernal Can Can, a lithograph by Doré depicting a scene from Orpheus

In *Tales of Hoffmann*, his swan song, Offenbach throws away the jester's dunce cap, and the ironic and sarcastic critic of Napoleon III's world mixes reality with fantasy. The satire is still there, but it takes the form of subtly cruel symbolism — falling in love with a performing mechanical doll; magic spectacles; mirrors that do not reflect images; and eternal drunkenness as an aid to forgetfulness. The music is evocative, and often powerful and ecstatic.

Figures from Tales of Hoffmann. *Offenbach always wanted to add to his fame by writing a grand opera.*

Johann Strauss Junior making his debut at Dormeyer's Casino in 1844 at nineteen.

THE VIENNESE WALTZ

Paris gaiety found its expression in Offenbach's operettas; Vienna's glittering society danced to the waltz tunes of the inimitable Strauss family. The history of the waltz is indeed a bit of Viennese history. Josef Lanner (1801–1843), Johann Strauss Senior (1804–1849), and his son Johann Junior (1825–1899) summarize the whole development of the form. Compared to these three important waltz composers, all the others are ephemeral.

A somewhat sentimental moonlit Romanticism is reflected in Lanner's works, which are soft and dreamy. In contrast, the elder Strauss is full of fire and life. After Lanner's death Strauss became the waltz

Johann Strauss, Senior, and Josef Lanner. They made the Viennese waltz world famous.

160

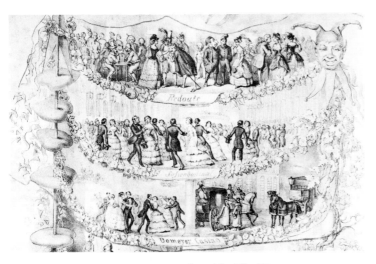

Dancing parties in Vienna's cafés. The Viennese went dance mad in the 1840's, and dance bands played in beer gardens, coffee houses, and restaurants.

The Beautiful Blue Danube, Austria's unofficial national anthem, was indifferently received at its first performance in Vienna, February 13, 1867.

Johann Strauss, Junior, at his desk. After he had retired from concert life, Strauss continued to compose dances and operettas, especially during the summer months at his villa at Ischl. He enjoyed the esteem of the most distinguished musicians. Composers like Wagner, Liszt, and Mahler recognized that his genius went far beyond the realm of light dance music.

king, but was immediately challenged by his son, who had his own band. It is remarkable, indeed, that the younger Strauss was able to retain the best from both older men, uniting Lanner's soft melodies with his father's vigorous rhythm and at the same time enlarging the form internally and externally. With unheard-of fecundity and facility the younger Strauss composed hundreds upon hundreds of dances. His art remained fresh and young, and this freshness safeguarded his waltzes from losing their original purpose, that of serving as dance music. Furthermore, Strauss also took the step that led from the ballroom to the theater, from the waltz to the Viennese operetta.

However, Strauss was not as lucky as Offenbach, who had two outstanding librettists in Meilhac and Halévy. Uncertain in his literary tastes, Strauss never selected a good libretto. Just the same, his fascinating musical talents triumphed in *Die Fledermaus (The Bat)*, which will remain the best German operetta. From the other of Strauss's sixteen operettas we should mention *The Gypsy Baron*. In this work, also, his endeavor to create a genuine comic opera was thwarted by a mediocre libretto; nonetheless, the operetta had a sensational success with a first run of eighty consecutive performances in Vienna.

161

César Franck at the organ in Sainte Clotilde, Paris. Franck would sit for a few minutes collecting his thoughts, then plunge into the most wonderful improvisations, working himself into a frenzy of excitement.

César Franck and the Resurgence of French Instrumental Music

The dominating position of grand opera in France in the second half of the 19th century was opposed by a school of composers who strove to re-establish French instrumental music to its rightful place. The undisputed leader of this group was César Franck (1822–1890). Since the general public had nothing but contempt for anything but operatic music, Franck spent fifty years of his life as an obscure teacher and organist. Then, after the first successful performances of some of his earlier works, he received a professorship at the Paris Conservatory, after which his creative spirit took new flight.

His life, devoid of the warmth of recognition, revolved within the confines of the narrow triangle formed by the organ of Sainte Clotilde's, the Conservatoire, and the French National Music Society. Success visited him only once, at the end of his life, when his string quartet was first performed in 1890. It is remarkable that all his important works were composed at an advanced age, in the '70s and '80s: an oratorio, *The Beatitudes*, several symphonic poems, organ and piano music, one celebrated symphony, and a few chamber works of which the Violin Sonata and Piano Quintet became well known. The significance of these works rests on the fact that they did attract, if belatedly, a group of disciples who saved absolute music from the dominance of the theater. It was not so much in their musical language that these works offered an example for the future, but rather in their proud and at the same time resigned artistic attitude. Franck's art is a demonstration against artistic demagoguery, and more an epilogue than a beginning; but its lesson was lasting, and he became the teacher of 20th-century French music.

Franck's numerous disciples formed an influential group which paid little heed to their contemporary colleagues. They cultivated a polyphonic style and wrote symphonies and quartets in classical formal patterns, while the rest of the musical world searched frantically for new forms. They stuck stubbornly to a leitmotivic and symphonic treatment of the lyric drama, while others did their utmost to throw off the Wagnerian yoke. It is understandable, then, that although it produced a good deal of pleasurable music, the school, except for Franck, wrote little of more than ephemeral value.

César Franck at the age of 40, when he still was unrecognized as a composer.

Gabriel Fauré is considered in his own country the embodiment of French musical genius. To the rest of the world many of Fauré's works seem pale. His songs are more universally admired.

Fauré's way of composing reminded critics of a woman doing a piece of embroidery. He was an impeccable craftsman.

The Followers of César Franck

One of the leading figures of the Franck school was Vincent d'Indy (1851–1931), a serious protagonist of the Liszt-Wagner-Franck heritage. A scion of the arch-Catholic petty nobility, he earnestly and fearlessly proclaimed his belief in medieval Catholicism in the midst of a skeptical secular French society. He founded the Schola Cantorum for the cultivation of old music, and announced in *Fervaal* the gospel of the Wagnerian music drama. But d'Indy was an apostle of the past, not of the future; this became the more noticeable the more the musicians around him became articulate. These musicians were not younger, either: Edouard Lalo (1823–1892), Emmanuel Chabrier (1841–1894), Gabriel Fauré (1845–1924) were of Franck's generation, but they were forward-looking spirits.

Vincent d'Indy was the most erudite of Franck's students and the master's biographer. His liking for contrapuntal construction was inspired by Bach.

Emmanuel Chabrier. Although he was attached to the Franck school, he was somewhat more boisterous than its other members.

164

Lalo's orchestral colorism was an almost symbolic demonstration of the musical melting pot that Paris had become by the end of the 19th century: for instance, his *Norwegian Rhapsody*, *Spanish Symphony*, and *Russian Concerto*. Indeed, the period produced a profusion of Persian songs, Algerian suites, Portuguese barcarolles, Russian caprices, and so on. What was needed was a composer of genius to rise above the sentimental salon atmosphere with genuine music, so that he could join Rimbaud, Maeterlinck, and Renoir on even terms. This composer was Claude Debussy.

Edouard Lalo. His strong sense for color in orchestration had a decisive influence on younger composers. His Spanish Symphony *established his reputation.*

Paul Dukas (1865–1935), best known for his symphonic poem, The Sorcerer's Apprentice. *He learned from everybody, but was able to maintain his own style.*

A concert in the Salle Pleyel in Paris with Sarasate as soloist. French orchestral music regained its rightful place with the founding of the Société Nationale de Musique.

Performances of oratorios by large choruses had been a fixture of the English musical scene since Handel's day. This popularity of oratorios was due in part to an English enthusiasm for sight-singing.

The Renaissance of Music in England: Parry, Sanford, and Elgar

THE VIGOROUS MUSICAL LIFE in England at the close of the 18th century continued into the beginning of the 19th. However, it could not hide the attrition of the native creative forces. Musical institutions flourished, and the universities continued to train their students in exemplary, if academic, fashion; but the decline of English music, in the narrower sense of the word, was complete.

This decline reached its nadir during the first part of Queen Victoria's reign. Then, in the last quarter of the century, a remarkable revival occurred. This musical renaissance was led mostly by two noted musicians, Sir Charles Hastings Hubert Parry (1848–1918) and Sir Charles Villiers Stanford (1852–1924). Parry was the profounder thinker of the two, and Stanford

the more accomplished musician. A new idea — setting the poetry of the great English writers, instead of manufactured librettos — was initiated in 1880 by Parry's *Prometheus Unbound* (Shelley), followed six years later by Stanford's *Revenge* (Tennyson). Parry was especially at home in choral works; the oratorios *Judith, King Saul,* and *Job* are representative examples of his music.

The non-British student of music passes over these works with polite praise, for indeed, with all the solid knowledge of the metier, the integrity and seriousness of the artists, the impact of this music is light. But for the Englishman, and for the student of English culture and civilization, there are values in this music, or rather in the life and work of Parry and Stanford. Both were men of great intellectual stature, professors re-

Sir Charles Hubert Parry and Sir Charles Villiers Stanford, leaders of the musical renaissance in Victorian England.

spectively in Oxford and Cambridge; they were friendly with the leaders of Victorian thought, and devoted themselves to their art and to the restoration of English music. Most of the composers who, after the turn of the century, revitalized English music came out of their school.

The 19th-century English revival of serious orchestral music was summarized by an earnest composer who occupies a position in England analogous to Fauré's position in France: Sir Edward Elgar (1857–1934). Elgar is one of the few English composers of the late Romantic era in whose music the Wagnerian and Brahmsian influences were fused with impressions gleaned from Liszt, Verdi, and Strauss. A Romantic-Classicist of solid musical attainment, Elgar is universally beloved in England; but this enthusiasm has not been communicated to the non-British public.

Although Elgar scored perhaps his greatest success in the traditionally British field of choral music with his oratorios and cantatas, he was equally accomplished as an instrumental composer. *The Dream of Ge-*

Sir Edward Elgar photographed by a friend. Elgar's oratorio, The Dream of Gerontius, *based on a text by Cardinal Newman, is considered his best work.*

rontius, written on a poem by Cardinal Newman, was followed by *The Apostles* and *The Kingdom.* The development of the instrumental composer was slower, for here Elgar had to overcome his youthful tendency toward salon music; yet he ended by creating the first modern English symphonies, which in many ways compare favorably with the works of Bruckner and Mahler. His orchestral virtuosity is remarkable; such works as *Enigma Variations, Cockaigne,* and especially the brilliant symphonic portrait, *Falstaff,* are landmarks in the immediate post-Romantic era.

Yet admired as he was, Elgar, who virtually ceased composing in 1919, did not create a school. The reason for this lies in his musical background, for he was self-taught, picking up his music wherever he found it. Moreover, this background was almost entirely German, and even the men who helped his career were Germans: Hans Richter, the conductor, A. E. Jäger, the publisher, and Richard Strauss, who greeted him as once Schumann had greeted Chopin. On the other hand, the rising school of British composers was seeking authentic native roots, which it found in Anglo-Celtic folksong and the Elizabethan madrigal — neither of which contributed to Elgar's development.

Sir Edward Elgar. He began as a society composer of romanticised salon music. Later his Enigma Variations *(1899) revealed an impressive craftsmanship and imagination.*

167

Sir William Gilbert (center) and Sir Arthur Sullivan (right). Their partnership, established in 1875, flourished under the guidance of Richard D'Oyly Carte, their impresario (left).

ENGLISH LIGHT OPERA: GILBERT AND SULLIVAN

The academic trend in English music faced a powerful countercurrent, the light opera, a peculiarly English genre. The music of Sir Arthur Sullivan (1842–1900) endeared itself to millions, not merely to an elite of academically trained connoisseurs. Sullivan succeeded in evolving, with the invaluable help of his able librettist, Sir William Gilbert (1836–1911), an inimitably British idiom that now typifies the late Victorian era.

A program of the 150th performance of Iolanthe *in Boston. American companies pirated Gilbert and Sullivan's works within a few months of their London successes.*

Figures from Pirates of Penzance.

168

Among Benjamin Franklin's many inventions was a mechanical form of musical glasses called the harmonica, which had a great vogue in Europe.

Lowell Mason, America's most influential pioneer in music education. In 1838, at his recommendation, music was made part of the curriculum in the Boston public schools.

Boston in the 1850's boasted an impressive music store. Music publishing flourished mainly through the efforts of Lowell Mason.

Music In America

THERE IS A certain similarity between English and American musical history in the 19th century. Both countries weathered foreign musical colonizations, conquered the invaders, and established their own artistic commonwealth; both reached their objectives through the deliberate planning and far-sighted work of enlightened musical statesmen.

New England, pre-eminent in literature, also took the lead in the field of music. Among the native musicians, Lowell Mason (1792–1872) emerged as the undisputed leader. He was more than a mere musician barely making a living (as a matter of fact, he earned the first American musical fortune); he was an educated American gentleman who made music a part of that foundation of American culture, the public school. The scion of an old American family, he hesitated for a time to abandon a business career as a banker. However, he realized it was within his power to shape the destiny of music in America, and once he made up his mind, nothing was able to withstand his determination. For some time he had to shoulder the expenses of his experiments himself, before he could convince school boards of the feasibility of teaching music to children. To spread the interest in music and its teaching, he established conventions of music teachers, gatherings in which teaching and the exchange of ideas were directed toward promoting the cause of music.

Toward the middle of the 19th century, all the sizable American cities had musical societies around which revolved an animated musical life. Several important new organizations came into being, such as the Philharmonic Orchestra in New York City, founded in 1842 by U. C. Hill (1802–1875). The first program played by this orchestra consisted of Beethoven's Fifth Symphony, Weber's *Oberon* overture, an overture by Kalliwoda, vocal excerpts from *Oberon, Fidelio,* and *The Abduction from the Seraglio,*

169

The Hutchinson Aeolians giving a concert in a frontier town. Singing families like the Hutchinsons, who came from New Hampshire, traveled all over the country.

Stephen Foster, the embodiment of American minstrelsy.

Hymn singing was a popular pastime on the American frontier. People in the west had a genuine enthusiasm for music.

a duet by Rossini, and — in the Continental manner — a piece of chamber music, a quintet by Hummel: a thoroughly artistic and progressive program, considerably superior to the fare offered by many contemporary European organizations.

Even opera flourished in America; the American public was familiar with the works of Mozart, Beethoven, Weber, Boieldieu, Auber, Donizetti, and Bellini. Ballads and popular songs were also greatly relished and a number of native composers, as well as some English musicians, produced them in quantity. But all of these, and most of the composers of art music as well, were overshadowed by Stephen Foster (1826–1864), the embodiment of American minstrelsy.

The Germania orchestra. This group of twenty-four German musicians came to New York in 1848, and gave more than nine hundred concerts all over the country.

With the growth of musical life in America, the parade of foreign virtuosi began. Singers — Jenny Lind, Henriette Sontag — and violinists — Ole Bull, Edward Reményi — came and conquered. But American virtuosi also began to find a public. Louis Moreau Gottschalk (1829–1869) measured up in every respect.

In the last quarter of the century, also, major symphony orchestras grew rapidly. The man who was largely responsible for the excellence and popularity of orchestral music was Theodore Thomas (1835–1905), who had come to America from Germany in early boyhood. Thomas traveled all over the country, leaving his impress on every musical organization of every city he visited, showing them the way, giving them the ideals to work for. Thomas was somewhat like Handel — an indefatigable man who met adversity with renewed energy and who was uncompromising in his artistic beliefs.

Hand in hand with the organization of a national concert life went the growth of creative musical talent. Many young American composers went to Germany to study in Leipzig, Weimar, or Dresden. These men were able to engage in the composition of the larger forms of music without apology or self-consciousness. They began to impress the old world of music, receiving encouragement and genuine praise and admiration even from Liszt. They were not giants; yet they as fully represented the culture of their homeland as did European composers, and they bear comparison with Europe's best.

Theodore Thomas conducting a concert in Central Park. Thomas traveled all through the country, organizing orchestras, choruses, and music festivals. He ended his career as conductor of the Chicago Symphony.

Louis Gottschalk, an American-born piano virtuoso. He was America's first matinée idol.

Ole Bull, a Norwegian violin virtuoso. Bull made five concert tours in United States.

Leopold de Meyer, a piano virtuoso whose performances reflected American taste for showmanship.

Jenny Lind. Her triumphal tour of 1850–1851, managed by Barnum, made her a fortune.

171

Edward MacDowell (1861-1908) was the first American composer of stature and world reputation. His studies in Germany, especially his work under the able Romantic symphonist Joachim Raff, left indelible marks on his musical personality, as did his meeting with Liszt. He liked the musical atmosphere in Germany so much that he lived in Wiesbaden for several years; but in 1888 he returned home and settled in Boston. His career advanced rapidly. The distinguished Venezuelan pianist, Teresa Carreño, and the famous Arthur Nikisch, then conductor of the Boston Symphony, became interested in his works and performed them with considerable frequency. When Columbia University established its chair of music in 1896, MacDowell was its first incumbent; however, academic life did not agree with him and he soon got embroiled with the faculty authorities, resigning in 1904. His life ended in tragic insanity.

MacDowell was an American composer more by virtue of his birth than by any genuine American qualities in his music. Nonetheless, he was a distinguished writer of the music of his time — music that could paint in colors. It is true that in MacDowell's colorfulness there was something of the hothouse and salon, but then most of the contemporary European musicians give the same impression, for they too liked the exotic. When MacDowell composed Indian suites he did not do so particularly because he was an American; rather, he was acting like his European colleagues who wrote music about India or Persia. MacDowell's music is well made, with good melodies and genuine inspiration, and works like the D Minor Piano Concerto compare favorably with similar compositions by Grieg.

Edward MacDowell at 18, when he was studying at the Paris Conservatory. Despite his studies there, MacDowell preferred the German masters.

MacDowell after his return to America in 1888, when he was at the height of his career.

MacDowell and his wife, who had been one of his students in Germany. In 1905 MacDowell's health began to break, and he died in 1908.

A drawing of Franz Liszt made by MacDowell when he visited the master at Weimar.

172

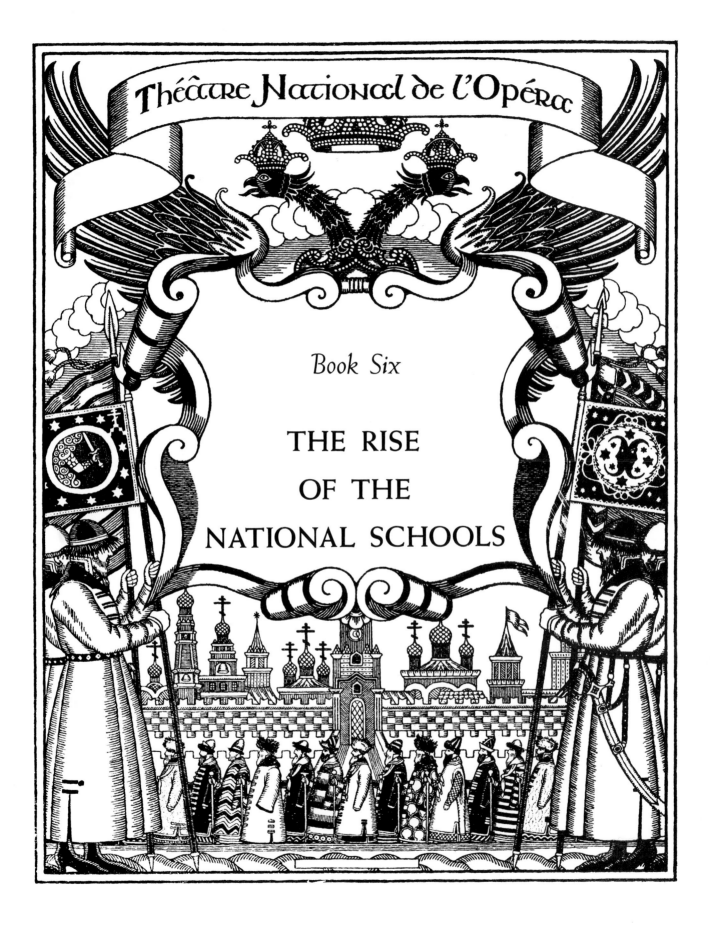

Théâtre National de l'Opéra

Book Six

THE RISE

OF THE

NATIONAL SCHOOLS

Folk dancers: Hungary, France, Austria.

The Influence of Folk Music

THE POST-WAGNERIAN PERIOD witnessed the disintegration of the Romantic schools, which had in various degrees dominated music throughout the second half of the 19th century. At this point a new element came into the world language of music. Certain countries which had previously made only token contributions to western art music now declared their independence; and the national schools of music came to the fore, as opposed to the more international styles of the 18th and earlier 19th centuries.

One of the important assets of all the national schools was the deliberate use of the elements of native folk music. Each folk music, because of its isolation from the mainstream of western art music, had preserved peculiar rhythms and harmonic idioms based on principles different from those commonly accepted. The composers of the new national schools strove to develop their own national dialects beyond the popular and the incidental into legitimate and autochthonous art works. There appeared then, almost miraculously, schools of Russian, Bohemian, or Scandinavian music; the music these schools produced greatly enriched the possibilities for musical expression.

The period of Nationalism in music was a short one. The peak of its influence was reached at the turn of the 19th century, after which Impressionism arose as its heir. Impressionism absorbed many of the elements of Nationalism and fused them into a new international style, the components of which suited Debussy, as well as a Falla, a Resphigi, or a Delius.

Russian playing dulcimer.

174

Michael Glinka, a founder of the school of Russian music. Although he was influenced by German and Italian musicians, he managed to develop in his operas a distinctly colorful and national style characterized by the use of vibrant, fresh folk tunes.

Nikolai Rimsky-Korsakov, the most productive, skillful, and admired member of the group of Russian nationalist composers called The Mighty Five. A lover of pageantry, he wrote flamboyant music, exotic rather than Russian in tone.

A scene from Glinka's second opera, Russlan and Ludmilla. *A monster is fought by Russlan, a Russian Siegfried.*

Glinka and The Five

THROUGHOUT THE HISTORY of Russian music two opposing tendencies are apparent: one to preserve national traits by excluding all western influences, the other to join with the west body and soul.

Along with other western importations, music found its way to Moscow when the wall that separated Russia from Europe began to crumble at the end of the 17th century. After this, and especially during the reigns of the Empresses Anne, Elisabeth, and Catherine, Italian music and opera contributed much to the glitter of the Russian court. The monopoly of Italian music was challenged in the early 19th century by an increasing Russian national consciousness. Voices began to be heard in favor of using Russian local color in the operatic works performed at court, and sensing a possible source of competition, the Italians tried to satisfy this desire by adapting some Russian tunes in their operas.

The constant vacillations between east and west that governed the progress of Russian music are evident in the life of Michael Ivanovich Glinka (1804–1857), the first significant figure in Russian music.

After studying with some German musicians residing in St. Petersburg, Glinka met Bellini and Donizetti when he spent a few years in Italy for his health. He went to Berlin for a more systematic musical training; then, back in Russia, Glinka came under the influence of the national literary movement, and his poet friends literally ordered him to compose *the* national opera. *A Life for the Tsar* was first performed in 1836. Critics and literati applauded it as a genuinely Russian work, but fashionable so-

ciety shrugged it off as "music of coachmen." A few years later, however, even the aristocracy thought that this work represented the beginnings of a national art music in Russia.

Glinka's next opera, *Russlan and Ludmilla* (1842), based on Pushkin's tale, did not fare so well as *A Life for the Tsar*, although from a musical point of view it shows progress and better workmanship. The disappointed composer again went abroad; in Paris he met Berlioz, and his association with the French program symphonist naturally resulted in symphonic works, of which *Kamarinskaya* is a notable example. Back again in Russia, Glinka's new operatic plans went awry and his last years were spent in a growing uncertainty about the rightful idiom of Russian national music.

The pseudo-folklike quality of Russian music of the early 19th century does not entirely disappear in Glinka's works; but it is superseded by a Romantic, popular tone that has a certain strength of style. Altogether the claim that Glinka invented a new form of opera cannot be sustained, for he accepted early grand opera with its arias and choruses; nevertheless, he filled these forms with his spirit and the spirit of his country.

Glinka was fairly well trained as a musician. Nonetheless, his feeling of technical inferiority prompted him to study in Italy and Germany.

The school of Russian music that overtly spurned the great musical heritage of the west, at least in theory, descended partly from that naturalism which appeared in literature with Gogol and in music with the pan-Slavic movement foreshadowed by Glinka. This school — a curious and colorful one — consisted of five musicians, living in St. Petersburg: Mili Alekseyevich Balakirev (1837–1910), who organized and taught the others; Alexander Porfirevich Borodin (1834–1887), professor of chemistry at the medical academy; Modest Petrovich Mussorgsky (1839–1881), an army officer; Nikolai Andreyevich Rimsky-Korsakov (1844–1908), a naval officer; and César Antonovich Cui (1835–1918), a military engineer.

Balakirev, although self-taught like the rest of The Five, was the only one of them who possessed the semblance of a professional knowledge of music. His genuine enthusiasm, as well as his initial instruction, was responsible for the careers of the other musicians, who ultimately surpassed him but who always regarded him affectionately as their teacher.

Borodin, although obviously an amateur in the noblest sense of the word, had a much more arresting personality. He had a rather modest musical output: two symphonies, two quartets, one opera, and a symphonic sketch, together with a few songs and smaller pieces; but all his pieces had wide popularity. The early symphony and

quartet are surprising mainly because they exist at all, composed as they were by a man barely familiar with the rudiments of composition. His later works, especially the opera *Prince Igor*, are at times beguiling in their fresh melodies and powerful choral scenes. Perhaps the most popular among Borodin's works is the symphonic sketch, *In the Steppes of Central Asia;* its impressionistic harmonic and orchestral idiom places its composer, as it were, between Liszt and Debussy.

Alexander Borodin. A benevolent man, he divided his busy life among research, teaching, and composing.

Prince Igor, *Borodin's masterwork, was unfinished at his death. He had worked on it for seventeen years. The* popular *Polovetsian Dances from* Prince Igor *were based on Borodin's researches on tribal melodies.*

177

Rimsky-Korsakov was the most celebrated and accomplished member of the
group. He was also interested in composing
Russian national music, but he set only the
beautiful fables which are indeed truly and
exclusively Russian in spirit. All the color,
pomp, and intoxication of the Slavic fairy
world are reflected in his scintillating, often
sensuously opulent orchestral and operatic
works; but the color and élan are like those
in the picture books which grownups read
with such pleasure to their children. Aside
from the folk tunes, there is a certain pau-
city of ideas in the most fetching of his orchestral poems, *Scheherazade;* it reminded
Debussy "more of a bazaar than of the
Orient."

Sultan Schahrian from Scheherazade.

Gogol's story The Golden
Cock *served Rimsky-Kor-
sakov as the basis for a
Russian fairy tale opera.*

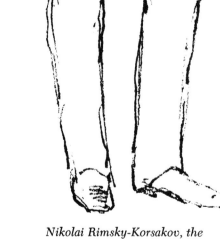

*Nikolai Rimsky-Korsakov, the
most versatile musician among
the Russian Five.*

Mussorgsky was the founder of modern musical realism and naturalism. The blind and fatal forces of life are real and menacing in Mussorgsky's world. His compositions were not merely pleasant Russian tunes arranged in nice bouquets. Like Wagner, Mussorgsky was a psychologist; and like his great literary colleagues, Gogol and Dostoyevsky, he was attracted to the forces and passions smoldering at the bottom of the human soul. The rendition of these instincts led Mussorgsky into spheres where no other Russian musician could follow. Only the great Russian writers were able to accompany him there.

Modest Mussorgsky in his early thirties. The composer's opera, Boris Godunov, *marked him as a daring and original experimenter.*

A design for a clock shaped like the hut of Baba Yaga, a witch of Russian folklore.

Three of the drawings by Victor Hartmann which inspired Mussorgsky's Pictures at an Exhibition.

Ballet of the Chickens, a stage scene for the ballet, Trilby.

The Great Gate of Kiev, topped by the emblem of Russia.

The false Dimitri, the pretender.

Boris: his fate is interwoven with the tragedy of the Russian people.

Feodor Chaliapin, the Russian basso famous for his playing of Boris.

Mussorgsky's psychological insight is embodied in *Boris Godunov*, the greatest musico-dramatic masterpiece of eastern Europe. *Boris* is not merely a tragedy of conscience; it is the universal tragedy of the Russian people cast as a musical folk drama. Mussorgsky penetrated into the spirit of his people with an elemental, fatelike force, conjuring up the problems of both the masses (the choruses) and the individuals (the songs) with an intensity of expression denied to all other Russian composers.

With the exception of Mussorgsky, there is little of the true Russian soul in the music of The Five, since these composers borrowed their musical language from the west. They established contact with the dying western Romantic movement, which they took for a nascent era; and modeling their own works on the late Romantic symphony, they fell heir to music in an outmoded form which could no longer adequately serve their idiom. This symphonic tradition of the west was also employed by Russia's first full-fledged professional composer — Peter Ilich Tchaikovsky.

Mussorgsky near the end of his career, when he struggled in vain against his alcoholism. He was unable to finish the music of Khovanshchina, his last opera; Rimsky-Korsakov completed it from Mussorgsky's sketches.

180

Peter Ilich Tchaikovsky

Tchaikovsky was totally unable in his first symphonies to find the symphonic tone. However, his artistic development in the latter part of his life was remarkable, and he ended his career with two symphonies which in popularity rival Beethoven's. Some of his thematic material is engaging and well-presented, but there is no trace of development in the symphonic sense. What he presents is merely a succession of repetitions and a sequence of climactic runs that often become hysterical. Then, in the Fifth and Sixth Symphonies, he exhibits an astounding growth in his stature as a com-

poser. The *Pathétique* (Sixth) Symphony — especially its lyric theme — is perhaps the most surefire piece of symphonic music ever composed. Every theme and motif is repeated time after time with little change; yet the composer succeeds in giving the impression of bona fide variations, largely through his masterful orchestration. Indeed, Tchaikovsky's handling of the orchestra in general is remarkable, ranging from delightful filigree work to blatant mass effects. It is undeniable that these large effects, perfect vehicles for conductorial extravagance, are the strongest reasons for his great popularity.

Tchaikovsky at the age of eight. He already showed musical talent.

In his early twenties, when he was studying with Rubinstein in St. Petersburg.

During his middle thirties, when he wrote his Fourth Symphony and Eugene Onegin.

Madame Von Meck, Tchaikovsky's beloved friend. She supported him, but they never met.

Tchaikovsky sitting in the garden of his country house at Klin near Moscow, now the Tchaikovsky State Museum.

Tchaikovsky does not belong in the company of the great in music; but neither can he be lightly dismissed. Russia never had a musician of stature who was more thoroughly international. His musical language, while cosmopolitan in technique, is not lacking in individuality; it expresses a powerful character with abstract but brilliant accents, in pictures that are not colorful, but shining. Altogether, it can be soaring, burning, and full of élan.

Tchaikovsky is thoroughly Russian in a less tangible aspect of Nationalism: the way he can pass, without warning, from the tearful Slavic sentimentalism of his melancholy into the most gross and brutal gaudiness. This duality appears in many of his works; for instance, the rousing Piano Concerto in B-flat, which pours out frenetic unison melodies at the very start while the piano pounds away impatiently until its turn

After his friendship with Madame Von Meck ended, Tchaikovsky was very dejected. He died of cholera in 1893 a few days after the première of his Symphonie Pathétique.

182

Eugene Onegin *was described by the composer as "lyric scenes in three acts." Tchaikovsky's music is not dramatic; rather, it delicately underscores sentiments and moods.*

Tatiana and Onegin

The Letter Scene

Onegin's Despair.

comes; the Violin Concerto, which opposes sensuous cantilena and offensively vulgar ornament; the ballets and suites, which on the whole are thoroughly enjoyable because of the restraint the composer imposed upon his orchestra and his vocabulary; and the symphonic poems or program overtures, noisy and hysterical beyond measure. These are all the works of a tragically perturbed soul, deeply stirred yet curiously bombastic, sincere yet overwrought — lacking the strength that comes from artistic discipline, but nonetheless musical to the core.

The Nutcracker Suite *was based on a children's story by Dumas père. It has remained Tchaikovsky's most popular work.*

Scene from Swan Lake, *as first staged in Moscow in 1877.*

Tchaikovsky's fame rests partly on his ballets. This music is animated by his genuine love of the dance.

183

Alexander Scriabin planned grandiose symphonies which were to utilize music, scent, and color.

Alexander Glazunov, the most productive composer of the post-Tchaikovsky generation.

Russians After Tchaikovsky

The generation of Russian composers which followed Tchaikovsky's, some members of which lived far into the 20th century, was again divided into two camps — this time not only by ideologies, but also geographically. The St. Petersburg group, led by Rimsky-Korsakov, was soon opposed by a Moscow school led by Sergei Taneyev, a pupil of Tchaikovsky. Among the Rimsky disciples were Alexander Glazunov (1865–1936) and Anatol Liadov (1866–1901). Glazunov, who produced his first symphony at an early age (he ceased to compose after 1905) was at first altogether under the influence of his master and the Mighty Five, but gradually developed a strong academic tendency. He overlaid Rimsky's homophonous

and melodic style with counterpoint as he became influenced by men like Brahms, whose imprint had been absent from Russian music. Liadov is of a lesser stature than Glazunov, but his invention is more original.

Of the members of the Moscow school, Alexander Scriabin (1872–1915) achieved both fame and notoriety. His whole art, indeed, his whole life, was a mere experiment. A modern mystic, he strove to achieve the universal music — a union of sound, color, drama, song, and · religion — but his new harmonic system proved only that a refurbishing of the tonal system was not enough to enable him to reach his goal.

Nikolai Medtner (1880–1951) is highly regarded, especially in England, as a fine piano and song composer, but it was Sergei Rachmaninov (1873–1943) who made the Taneyev group world famous. Rachmaninov was a colorful pianist of suggestive power and dramatic imagination, qualities that are also reflected in his compositions. His Prelude in C-sharp Minor, which became one of the most celebrated piano pieces in the world, was written when he was 19. His Second Piano Concerto became the most popular work of its kind in the 20th century. This able and devoted musician, despite the fact that he lived into our time, was completely wedded to the world of Tchaikovsky, to 19th-century Romanticism. His gestures are expansive and passionate, his melodies melancholy, and his canvas of large proportions. His popularity in Russia and in the English-speaking countries remains unimpaired, but the rest of Europe never took to him.

Sergei Rachmaninov — a drawing by Pasternak. His compositions rarely deviate from classic forms and are pervaded by melancholy.

Lyricists of the Homeland: Smetana and Dvořák

THE SO-CALLED Viennese school had among its members many Czech and German-Bohemian musicians. These men were prominent in developing the instrumental lyricism that preceded Schubert.

Bohemia was a highly musical country. During the long Austro-German rule, Bohemian music was part of German music, and Bohemian musicians were one branch of German musical history. The 19th-century national orientation separated Bohemia from the Austrian musical orbit, and the move toward a national Bohemian music was prepared by theoreticians, educators, and musicians. Then, in Bedřich Smetana (1824-1884) and Antonin Dvořák (1841–1904), Bohemia found native composers equal to those of the neighboring musical empires.

When the music of the Bohemians is compared to that of the contemporary Russian and other national schools, the natural ease and unaffected spontaneity with which the Czechs move in their idiom is immediately apparent. Their musicianship is always sound and thoroughly workmanlike even in the lesser members of the school.

Bedřich Smetana is called the "father of Czech music," inasmuch as he was the first to draw deliberately on the source of Bohemian folk music. He abandoned the well-tried devices of international grand opera and utilized themes based on the tales and the life of his homeland. Smetana wrote eight works for the lyric stage, of which, significantly, only the comic examples were successful — in these pieces the great treasure of Bohemian folk song and dance could be used without giving the impression of mere exoticism. *The Bartered Bride* (1866) will remain one of the most engaging pieces in the repertory of the lyric stage.

Smetana began work as a symphonist after his experiences with opera, and he wrote an orchestral epic, the six cantos of which depicted six aspects of the Bohemian countryside. Completely steeped in the history of Smetana's nation, in its heroes, mountains, valleys, and streams, *Ma Vlast (My Country)* is a captivating narrative which will remain an oasis in the program music literature of the late Romantic era.

Bedřich Smetana in the 1860's, after he had successfully launched the Czech National Theatre in Prague.

Characters from Smetana's Bartered Bride. *This folk opera reflected Bohemia's desire for independence.*

185

Antonin Dvořák rejuvenated traditional forms with melodies from songs and dances of his country.

Antonin Dvořák lacked Smetana's dramatic strength and descriptive talents; but his chamber music reflected an ample and fertile musical imagination, healthy temperament, a simple yet by no means shallow sentiment and inventiveness, and a balanced sense of form. Everyone liked his music, and everyone was satisfied with it except Dvořák himself, who felt that the world viewed him less as an individual composer in his own right than as a representative of the new music of Bohemia.

Therefore, Dvořák resolved to present his personality in sharper relief by using materials and subjects untouched by his countrymen, which he could shape by the force of his own musical imagination. Thus the musician who for a quarter of a century was numbered among the practitioners of absolute music joined the ranks of the program musicians. He did not succeed in this field despite his ardor and seriousness of purpose; for his was an essentially naïve nature, not equal to the task of the greatness his subjects demanded.

Dvořák affords convincing proof for the idea that nationality may give the composer a material world, but great and lasting works are produced only if the content arises from the depths of a positive personality — in which case the geographical and ethnic restrictions are immediately overcome. The best illustration is the great and deserved popularity of Dvořák's Fifth Symphony, *From the New World*, the inspiration for which came from his stay in America from 1892 to 1893.

Czech couple dancing Dvořák's Slavonic Dances.

The first performance of Dvořák's most famous symphony, From the New World, *at Carnegie Hall, December, 1893. This work was inspired by Dvořák's impressions of America.*

Music of the North

THE CHARACTER of the national music of the Scandinavian countries is entirely different from that of Slavonic music. In richness and originality northern folk music is scarcely surpassed by the music of any other nation; nonetheless, the music of northern Europe is not really national — merely nationally colored. Almost all the Scandinavian composers of the Romantic era studied in Leipzig, Dresden, and Berlin, and brought home the spirit of German Romanticism which they adapted to their particular needs. For instance, the representative composer of Denmark, Niels Gade (1817–1890) was entirely submerged in the spirit of the Leipzig composers, especially Mendelssohn and Schumann.

Of the Norwegian musicians Halfdan Kjerulf (1815–1869) was among the first to emphasize the Norwegian tone with songs and choruses that employed folklore elements. This modest music has the virtue of staying within self-imposed limits; but later Norwegians, Johan Svendsen (1840–1911) and Christian Sinding (b.1856), attempted to acclimatize the idioms of Berlioz and of the neo-German school. The music of both these composers is pleasing and workmanlike, but cosmopolitan and shallow, without a marked profile.

Of a much more positive nature is the musicianship of Edvard Hagerup Grieg (1843–1907), who was largely responsible for the vogue of Scandinavian music in Europe and America. At first he was carried by the same Romantic current that dominated Gade's works. In fact, he belonged to the same Leipzig circle that nurtured all other Scandinavian composers; but he then came under the influence of a very gifted musician, Richard Nordraak (1842–1866), who introduced him to the folk music of Norway. Grieg's music then changed, and he began to compose piano pieces and songs which were delicate and appealing. Much of his chamber music is also under the influence of this lyricism, and there are some fine genre scenes among them. However, the large forms are wanting, for Grieg lacked not only the concentration but even the will to master architectural construction; his ideas are too lyric and are quickly lost in mere sequential miniature work. His soft disposition was combined with the austere and stark dramatic personality of Ibsen in one notable score, the incidental music to *Peer Gynt;* in this work the softness of the composer's music provides a welcome contrast to the play, which is overwrought with ideas and forebodings.

Edvard Grieg shortly after his graduation from Leipzig Conservatory. He was only twenty-five when he wrote his Piano Concerto in A Minor.

Grieg playing in a cabin on his estate, Troldhaugen, near the Stardanger Fjord.

Grieg was a small and fragile man, hardly five feet tall; yet his appearance was impressive.

Grieg accompanying his wife, Nina Hagerup, for whom he wrote one of the world's best-known songs: I Love Thee.

JEAN SIBELIUS: HEROIC VISIONS OF FINLAND'S PAST

Sibelius in his early thirties. After studying in Berlin and Vienna, he returned to Finland to join the national art movement.

Jean Sibelius (1865–1957) was like Robinson Crusoe on his island, an island set in the wide sea of the post-Romantic era. He let the fantasies of Tschaikovsky and others feed his imagination, but despite some initial hesitation, he did not let himself be carried away by them. Granted an exceptional span of life and blessed with a rugged physique, the Finnish master literally outlived his own time, ceased composing decades before his death, and enjoyed the rare privilege of living to see his work recognized after the usual lag of a generation or two. Thus Sibelius became a living legend, a popular hero not only in little Finland but in the whole world.

In Finland Sibelius is worshipped as the founder of a musical culture that has become an integral part of western art; and indeed, his art represents the greatest musical manifestation of Finnish civilization, being deeply rooted in the history of his northern homeland. Sibelius's music extols his nation's mythical dreams in great symphonic tableaus and in seven large symphonies which occupy an important position in the more recent symphonic literature. The Finnish national epic, *Kalevala*, furnished a magnificent frame for his contemplative and heroic musical visions, as well as for his engaging and profound poetry of nature. In the later symphonies especially, Sibelius gives proof of a capacity for tense imaginative expression, growing out of, but transcending, the lyrical fancy of his earlier works.

Sibelius at work in his country house at Järvenpää. His genius was inspired by stories of Finland's heroic past.

189

Sibelius and his work are surrounded in certain quarters, particularly in England and the United States, with an aura of devotion which makes it difficult to estimate the nature of his gifts. More than one writer in these two countries (although nobody in the rest of Europe) has declared him to be one of the very greatest of symphonists, rivalling Beethoven and Brahms. This is, of course, an untenable position. Sibelius's limitations must be recognized even at the risk of seeming ungracious, because unnoticed they lead to serious error.

The national formula has its dangers. When a composer is saturated, as Sibelius was, with the shapes, sights, smells, speech, and characteristics of a country, he may sometimes be tempted to clothe a not very satisfactory frame with all these telling appurtenances. As a matter of fact, Sibelius is often inclined to make ritual mystery out of what is perhaps no more than mystification. At times his music unfolds like a gentle, unsensational movie; at others, it is centrifugal and the component parts have a tendency to

Scene from the Finnish epic Kalevala: *The hero Lemminkäinen, murdered near the River of Death, is revived by his mother. Sibelius based his* Four Legends *on this story and others from Finland's past.*

spread outward. One might say that the true significance of his work lies far more in its tone and atmosphere than in the intrinsic value of its melodic, harmonic, or formal qualities.

He must have felt that the framework of national themes were too general and a little loose for a lonely man; and the presence of a classically ordered, almost severe design is increasingly felt in his later symphonies. The freely flowing romantic lyricism of his youth becomes more concentrated, more mature, more expressive, and one is aware of a certain transcendent seriousness. Such self-criticism is rare in the annals of art; and the uncompromising Sibelius has earned a place in the history of music that no one else can claim.

Book Seven

TOWARD IMPRESSIONISM

Signac: Port of La Rochelle.

In Impressionist painting, outlines dissolve into an iridescent haze. Music too abandoned rigid forms, and began to conjure up the flow of mood.

Renoir: The Daughters of Augusta Holmès. *Impressionism abandoned the heroic gesture of the Romantics, and set out to recreate momentary impressions.*

Stéphane Mallarmé, one *of the leaders of Symbolism. He helped Debussy develop the esthetics of Impressionist music.*

New Notions of Tonality

THE END OF THE 19th century witnessed a tremendous upheaval, intellectual, social, moral, and artistic, directed sharply against the tenets of Romanticism. There was a reversal in the ideas of pictorial space, of form, and of tonality, a reversal which paralleled similar re-evaluations of the ideas of space and time which were occurring in modern physics. Impressionism in the visual arts represents the first stage in the dissolution of the concept of a geometrically constructed pictorial space, although artists still adhered to the system of optical projection originated in the Renaissance. In a similar fashion, music emancipated itself from the major-minor system of tonality imposed upon it since Renaissance times.

The strongest incentive toward a new tonal sense came from Liszt. He was the first to employ a "neutral tonality" based on the whole-tone scale; this tonality subsequently became one of the earmarks of the Impressionist style. To this widening of the tonal sense was added the use of the medieval ecclesiastical scales and the folk idioms of the national schools, all contributing first to an extension and reorganization of the old system and later to its disintegration.

In the course of this development into Impressionism, the old symphonic forms were abandoned. The post-Romantic and Impressionist schools sought form in the unity of mood. Their musical idiom does not operate with isolated thematic material, as did the idioms of the Classic and Romantic periods, but with motives which are developed without definite pauses into a universal fabric of endless melody. Thus in Impressionist music, the symphony and the sonata become extended fantasies which attempt to combine a freely handled, predominantly lyric fabric with the pattern of the sonata form, now meaningless. Instead of the clear articulation of a musical phrase, swinging, undulating repetitions are used. In the same way that pointillist painters juxtaposed colored dots to create a definite color sensation in the eye of the beholder, composers combined many far-removed intervals to create a vibrating, vacillating, glimmering sound complex, trembling and nervous, which caressed the senses.

In spite of these new approaches, post-Wagnerian music was in a state of confusion. The best minds either exhausted themselves in the search for a breach in the Wagnerian wall, deceived themselves and the world with virtuoso verbosity, or produced works which were belligerent professions of faith in the cultural weapons of old Europe, made at a time when these weapons had already been discarded by the new armies of modern music.

193

Mahler in his early twenties, when he was conducting in small Austrian opera houses.

In the 1890's, Mahler was conducting in Hamburg and working on his early symphonies.

Gustav Mahler and the Monumental

THE REPRESENTATIVE COMPOSERS of post-Wagnerian pre-Impressionist music were Gustav Mahler (1860–1911), Max Reger (1873–1916), and Richard Strauss (1864–1949), three musicians who stand above a multitude of minor figures. A fourth representative composer, Hugo Wolf (1860–1903), applied his somewhat feverish energy exclusively to writing songs. All these men typify the prevailing tendencies and embody the spirit of the dying 19th century without appreciably becoming part of the 20th, although one of them, Strauss, lived until 1949.

These post-Romantics, with the exception of Wolf, believed that a direct ratio existed between the size of the apparatus of expression and the ideas to be expressed. They were convinced that by utilizing all available tonal resources they could create compositions of equivalent artistic value. The composer who believed this most firmly was Gustav Mahler. His attitude toward art was not only novel; it had greatness. It was

not that of the 20th-century "orchestrator who believes in his métier only, but that of an artistic personality of uncompromising earnestness and integrity.

Mahler strove for monumentality, and to this end he gathered and used every available means at his disposal. It cannot be denied that the performance of such a work as his Eighth Symphony has something grandiose about it. However, the performance itself cannot be separated from the work, which suffers greatly when, as in recordings, the performing apparatus is not visible — for the external presentation indicates the inner musical construction. In the background there is a great organ; in front of it, on platforms, a large choir of children; at a somewhat lower level, several hundred male singers; then, grouped around two pianos, two large female choirs. In the middle of all this sits a gigantic orchestra, comprising, in addition to all varieties of modern orchestral instruments in multiple numbers, a piano, a harmonium, a mandolin, bells,

Glockenspiele, and a wide variety of percussion instruments — the whole capped by a special brass choir.

It is sad, however, to be compelled to admit, in the face of the deployment and adroit handling of such forces, of such unsparing energy, inexorable will, and intellectual effort, that the only great thing in these creations is the intention. The composer of these gigantic works was, at the bottom of his heart, a lyricist; and he founders in the epic vastness of the symphony. Often there are some convincing and spellbinding details, but these cannot cover the lack of cohesion and aesthetic unity.

As a conductor Mahler was relentless and often ruthless. His perfectionism gained him the enmity of performers, but the adulation of the audience.

Statue by Rodin in the Vienna State Opera.

Mahler on his way to the Vienna State Opera. His work there from 1897 to 1907 was the highpoint of his conducting career.

195

Hugo Wolf: Master of Modern Song

IN THE WORKS of Gustav Mahler, songs were pivotal. He turned poems into songs, and the songs in turn inspired the themes and moods of his symphonies. Yet it was not in Mahler's gigantic symphonies but in the more modest, more intense songs of Hugo Wolf that post-Romantic vocal art reached its apex.

Hugo Wolf was a child of his era, a tragic phenomenon of the declining century. He took his themes from the spiritual store of German Classicism, elaborating them in a peculiarly nervous and sophisticated manner. He tried to combine Schumann's lyricism with the declamatory style of the Wagnerian circle, using their chromatic-enharmonic idiom to the point of saturation. The scale of Wolf's sentiments is truly limitless, ranging from the most delicate mirth to religious submission, expressed with almost impressionistic lightness of touch, yet at times capable of eruptive force.

The Romantic song composer who was inspired by a poem transformed it into a song; this song was no longer the property of the poet. Wolf wanted something else. He did not recast mood and idea, but attempted to guide the listener's soul toward the text of the poem; music was used only to enhance the poem. He was a rhapsodist, albeit a rhapsodist who used his instrument not only for the purpose of accompaniment but as an independent medium for creating moods. The musical essence of the composition is in the piano part, and it was entirely proper for him to call his works "Songs for voice and piano," and not "Songs with piano accompaniment." Wolf's accompaniment is musically independent, free from the vocal part, yet entirely subordinated to the text. He used the piano as Wagner used his orchestra; and his piano ruled the song as Wagner's orchestra ruled the stage.

Hugo Wolf in 1889. By this time he had achieved some success with his song cycle based on poems by Mörike.

A scene from Wolf's opera, The Corregidor.

During a private recital before the Vienna Wagner Association, Hugo Wolf discusses new songs.

196

Reger at work: He strove valiantly to fuse the styles of Bach and Brahms.

By jumping the hurdle of tonality, Reger became an early trail blazer for modernism.

Reger combined the career of composer, teacher, and virtuoso. He also conducted the famous ducal orchestra of Meiningen.

Max Reger:
A Return to Polyphony

THE LEADER of the so-called contrapuntal school, Max Reger, embodies another aspect of the confusion at the end of the 19th century. His creative force owed more to technique than inspiration. He tried to establish contact with the great masters of Baroque counterpoint, but his counterpoint is largely a pseudo-polyphony. He carried chromatic contrapuntal subjects to the ultimate dissolution; and in so doing he blazed the trail for modern composers.

Having mastered counterpoint, Reger was able to write successful variations on borrowed themes, chorale preludes, and other works. As a rule, these variations are not metamorphoses of the original's spiritual and poetic content, but merely musical playing with given material. However, even these compositions often became incoherent in their tonality, and eternal chromatic modulations. There is honest effort, but little creative spark in most of his music.

Reger sought endlessly and in vain for the ideals that once animated the great masters of the German past. His constant questing did not permit him to develop an art with deep roots, and it made his music feverish and unhealthy. That is why Reger's works, no matter how interesting and remarkable, affect a listener's nerves rather than his soul.

Young Richard Strauss.

Franz Strauss, Richard's father, was a famous horn virtuoso. Richard composed a horn concerto for him.

Richard Strauss: Wizard of the Orchestra

WHILE OTHER COMPOSERS tortured themselves with the problems of life and art, Richard Strauss freed himself from all mystical and metaphysical ties and proceeded to utilize everything the century had produced in a technical synthesis, thus becoming the greatest virtuoso and technician of the declining century. ("Virtuoso" is not used here in a derogatory sense — for virtuosity carried to such a degree is art.) It is true that in his synthesis there is nothing of the spiritual content of Classicism and Romanticism, none of their problems, none of their joys. He explored all styles with gusto, always emerging, unlike Mahler, unscathed; instead of being burdened with memories, he made off with a bag of new tricks, for Strauss had the powerful physique and the rhetorical skill of a tribune of the people. He had no scruples of conscience to bother him, no preconceived theories, no feeling of social responsibility, no commitment to a univer-

sal art — for he was a musician who liked music and accepted the world as it is.

The uselessness of writing symphonies, quartets, or piano sonatas was apparent to Strauss after a few essays in those media; his instinct warned him of the impossibility of reconciling the ideas and ideals of the music of his time with these inherited forms. The great problem of form that defeated most of his contemporaries Strauss solved by writing his music around programs whose episodes he marked with characteristic motives fathered by the Wagnerian system. This was not an eminently musical solution, for it is impossible to impute to music expressions of fate *(Death and Transfiguration)* or experience *(The Life of a Hero)*. Yet Strauss's solution proved to be more workable than the pseudo-sonatas and was, of course, much more readily intelligible to everyone.

Strauss carried the Wagnerian technique to its apogee; compared to him all the other followers of Bayreuth seem victims rather than disciples.

Strauss as a young conductor at Weimar rehearsing a Humperdinck opera. Von Bülow selected him for this important post.

A medieval folk figure comes to life in Strauss' score, Till Eulenspiegel's Merry Pranks.

In Don Quixote Strauss deftly expressed the admixture of humor and pathos in Cervantes' immortal hero.

In his operas Strauss endeavored to combine Wagnerian music drama with the Mozartean opera. Needless to say, this was a dangerous undertaking, and although his prodigious technical skill succeeded in converting the recitative into a swiftly moving orchestral fabric, and the aria into a broad cantilena, Strauss's orchestra always remains in undisputed control, dictating mood as well as form. In fact, he really dramatized the symphonic poem, and his operas are orchestra operas even more than are Wagner's.

Der Rosenkavalier (The Knight of the Rose; 1911) is an attempt at pure operatic music-making in the 18th-century sense. The operas he had written before this had been heavy with orgiastic revelry, with nothing of the charm of whisper, insinuation, delicacy, and make-believe; but in *Rosenkavalier* Strauss wanted to recapture the spirit of Mozart's — and the other Strauss's — Vienna. And he almost succeeded — almost, because the charm is a bit faded, and the gracefulness a bit forced; but he did give us an unquestioned masterpiece.

Instead of the Freudian nightmares of *Salome* and *Elektra, Rosenkavalier* conjures up with considerable skill the frivolous, elegant, and at times slightly melancholy world of old Vienna. Hofmannsthal's libretto is excellent, the characters are sympathetic, and they are given plenty of chances to sing. The orchestra is handled with utter brilliance, yet it does not dominate the stage. This opera is Strauss's most engaging and viable stage work; nothing he composed afterwards can be compared to it.

The Strauss family: Richard, Pauline and son Franz. In 1894 Strauss married Pauline de Ahna, prima donna of his opera, Guntram.

199

Moreau's painting of Salome inspired Oscar Wilde to write his play, Salome, *which Strauss used as his libretto.*

Mary Garden as Salome. When this opera was first performed in 1905, it shocked the musical world.

Richard Strauss at a rehearsal of Electra.

Strauss and his librettist, Hugo von Hof-mannsthal. Hofmannsthal provided Strauss with six librettos, from 1909 to 1934.

Ochs auf Lerchenau.

Characters from Der Rosenkavalier.

Octavian: the presenta-tion of the rose.

Strauss conducting in the 1930's. His leadership, undisputed in the early 20th century, rapidly declined after the advent of Hitler. He died shortly after the end of the war.

Puccini in the early 1890's. His opera Manon Lescaut, *performed in Turin in 1893, had made him famous.*

A caricature of Puccini done in 1898.

Puccini at his studio at Torre del Lago, the country home he loved. He is buried in a crypt behind the piano.

Puccini with Illica and Giacosa, his librettists, who gave him texts that have made "the world weep."

Tosca, *Puccini's most dramatic opera, with its story of torture, murder and suicide. (Ricordi Archive)*

Costume sketches for La Bohème, *which had its première in Turin in 1896 under the baton of the twenty-nine year old Toscanini.*

Giacomo Puccini: Genius of the Theatre

S TRAUSS'S OPERA remained controversial — but the work of Giacomo Puccini was enthusiastically accepted by the public. A full-blooded opera composer, more familiar than any one of his contemporaries with the secrets of theatrical effect and success, he became the idol of the opera-going world. His sure instinct — evident even in the selection of his libretti — was the substantial heritage bequeathed to him by the great past of Italian opera. Yet Puccini did not remain unconditionally faithful to the tenets of this great tradition. He learned from Verdi the externals rather than the essence; and from the school of verismo he appropriated only a love of brutal, often trivial effects.

Still, his wonderful sense for new colors, ideas, tricks, and above all his rich melodic invention, and clever but unostentatious orchestration attest to the existence of a born and distinguished artist. The exotic color which gradually veiled his stage, the burlesque, bizarre, and grotesque elements he salvaged from the old and inexhaustible mine of the *opera buffa*, he handled as a real master.

Nonetheless, what is ardent passion on Verdi's stage is more like hysteria on Puccini's. The youthful ardor, verve, and lyricism of *La Bohème* were soon drowned in enervating refinement; in *Tosca* and *Madame Butterfly* the costumes are more noticeable, as is the forced use of local color, but these works still make good theater and are essentially operatic. Toward the end of his life Puccini again found himself in the macabre but virtuoso humor of *Gianni Schicchi*, a modern *opera buffa* which shows deep insight into the problems of the musical stage.

Geraldine Farrar, as Cio-Cio-San in the American première of Madame Butterfly *in 1907.*

The Girl of the Golden West, *starring Caruso, was performed at the Metropolitan Opera in 1910, with limited success.*

203

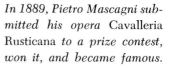

Puccini described himself as a "mighty hunter of wild fowl, opera librettos, and attractive women." He also loved cars and motor boats.

VERISMO'S MINOR MASTERS

Verismo reached its peak in Puccini's operas. Two of his contemporaries, Pietro Mascagni (1863–1945) and Ruggiero Leoncavallo (1858–1910), produced operas in a similar style, and were considered important figures in their lifetime. Yet only one short work of each of these composers is still a part of today's repertory. Although *Cavalleria Rusticana* and *Pagliacci* have many things in common and are equally popular, they represent two very different musical personalities. Mascagni's swiftly moving Sicilian peasant drama shows a real dramatic musical temperament, and although the naturalism of the libretto is powerful, there is still a good deal of the melodic pathos of late Romanticism. Leoncavallo's verism is much more brutal and lacking in refinement; but there is a certain innate coarse power in his drama.

In 1889, Pietro Mascagni submitted his opera Cavalleria Rusticana *to a prize contest, won it, and became famous.*

The opening scene of Pagliacci, *in which the strolling players arrive, led by Canio. Leoncavallo wrote his own libretto.*

204

Impressionism: Claude Debussy, the Flagbearer

THE TERM "IMPRESSIONISM" is generally applied to the fine arts; but, as usual, music and poetry, philosophy and ethics, the thinking and acting of a whole period, echo similar tendencies. Impressionism was a style in which moods were not merely dominating but enhanced by a preference for the accidental, the uncontrollable, the unique; it was thus especially suitable for music. Led by French musicians, musical Impressionism soon recruited an international following around its banner, with Claude Debussy (1862–1918) the flag-bearer.

Erik Satie. He admonished Debussy not to imitate the overblown Wagnerian forms, but to express the French spirit in concise, luminous pieces.

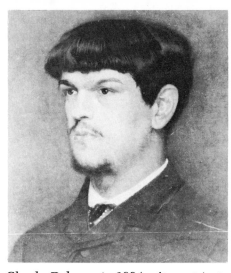

Claude Debussy in 1884, after a trip to Italy as the recipient of the Prix de Rome. Always defiant, he found the atmosphere in Italy too stifling.

The new musical style evolved from the disintegrating post-Romantic and national schools, used certain elements in the music of Bizet, Franck, Wagner, Grieg, Borodin, and Mussorgsky, and reacted sympathetically to influences emanating from contemporary poetry and painting. Its international character is well illustrated in the membership of the school, which included among others, Maurice Ravel (1875–1937), Cyril Scott (b.1879), Frederick Delius (1862–1934), Ottorino Respighi (1869–1936), and Manuel de Falla (b.1876).

The leader of the school, Claude Achille Debussy, at the beginning of his career vacillated between the two extremes that dominated French musical life: Massenet and Wagner. In the eighties the Wagnerian ikon was turned toward the wall, for through the work of his friends, Erik Satie and Ernest Chausson, he realized that there was a way to dispel the Bayreuth magic.

He met the leading exponents of Impressionist and Symbolist poetry and painting, and made the great discovery that there had once been a French art such as he dreamed about, the art of Couperin and Rameau. This discovery gave direction to his instincts, and having found his voice, he astounded the world with an orchestral prelude to Mallarmé's poem *The Afternoon of a Faun*. This prelude was immediately followed by a string quartet, and later by a lyric drama, *Pelléas and Melisande*, works

which confirmed his great and original talent. But it took many years of struggle before the private cause of a little band of admirers assumed the aspect of a world-wide movement of Impressionist music.

Debussy approximated Cézanne's palette with his orchestra and piano, Verlaine's musical verse with his poetic recitation. At the same time he was able to endow this dazzling game of light and shadow with life and poetic expression. His late works are in a noble and distilled style. Their nature still remains to be grasped, as can be seen from the rather ambiguous adjective "neoclassic" which musical writers have bestowed upon them.

A poster by Valentine Gross for the ballet The Afternoon of a Faun, *with Nijinsky.*

206

Debussy in 1874, at the age of twelve, when he entered the Paris Conservatory.

In 1880. As the pianist in Madame von Meck's trio, he traveled through Russia and Italy.

About 1895 in the house of his friend, Pierre Louys. He wrote his string quartet about this time.

Debussy at the piano studying with his friends Mussorgsky's Boris Godunov, *a work that deeply influenced Debussy's style, and that of his contemporaries.*

In 1904, the year he completed The Sea, *Debussy explained that this work was not a wave by wave description of the sea, but rather an evocation of its magic and mystery.*

A poster design for the first performance of
Pelléas and Mélisande, *April 30, 1902.*

Mary Garden in the first performance of
Pelléas and Mélisande. *She had a great
share in the opera's eventual success.*

Debussy wrote symphonic poems, chamber music, and songs throughout his life, and he found new tones, new forms, and new expressions for all of them. Opera tempted him only once. *Pelléas and Mélisande,* based on a libretto by Maeterlinck, does not resemble any other opera ever performed in a theater. It is absolutely original in its endeavor to repudiate any melodic design, and the singing is reduced to psalmodic declamation which comes very close to natural spoken language. The orchestra follows the text almost word for word and excels in the descriptive passages; but the work always remains music of the poet and of an Impressionist painter; it is never music of a thinker.

*A cartoon of Debussy
setting aflame the ven-
erable bastion of music.*

Title lithograph by Raoul Dufy for Le Tombeau de Debussy, *a memorial volume of compositions by the important representatives of modern music.*

208

Maurice Ravel: Elegant Miniaturist

Ravel in 1912, with Nijinsky, studying the score of the ballet Daphnis and Chloe, *which Nijinsky choreographed.*

Maurice Ravel (right) in 1902, with Ricardo Viñes. This Spanish pianist was the foremost interpreter of Ravel's piano music.

Unlike Debussy, with whom he is conventionally linked, Maurice Ravel (1875–1937) was not an intuitive composer. Debussy is full of instinct and feeling; everything that Ravel does is conscious and calculated. Yet it would be unjust to see in him nothing but a supreme master of musical craftsmanship for there is a great deal of imagination and humor in his work. Although he lacks the profound traits of the French spirit, he possesses other, more popular, French characteristics, such as elegance, wit, and sparkle, in abundance. His natural elegance is reflected in a particular, many-sided, and brilliant musical language, which varies from work to work yet remains positive and personal.

When one contemplates such works as *Gaspard de la Nuit* (piano suite), *L'Heure Espagnole* (opera), *Chansons Madécasses* (songs), or *La Valse* (orchestral fantasy) one realizes that each of them represents a date in recent French musical history. A few measures suffice to identify Ravel as their composer and yet they resemble one another only superficially. In the end one becomes aware of his far-reaching influence upon his confreres, an influence from which some of them — for instance, Jacques Ibert — could hardly liberate themselves.

The Teacup in Ravel's ballet The Bewitched Child. *Design by Aline Bernstein for the New York City Opera Ballet.*

A La Scala performance of Ravel's L'Heure Espagnole, *an amusing one-act comic opera, set in a watchmaker's shop. Clocks whizz, tick, and whirr through the score.*

Yet when one examines Ravel's music closely it is difficult to see what made it so attractive and influential. Its principal characteristics are a sure handling of form, a cold but colorful radiance, a wonderfully musicianly continuity. At the same time, the nervous alternation of a great variety of effects — we may even say tricks — and especially the rationally deliberate planning are obvious. A musical personality like Ravel's eventually seeks the natural outlet for the virtuoso bravura of a juggler's technique: the miniature. And indeed, Ravel **was** particularly devoted to short individual orchestral pieces (his suites are a series of these), and to rapidly moving, beautifully coordinated short operas. The finely ironical, at times lightly sentimental, veiled lyricism of his songs and piano pieces also betrays the miniaturist.

Ravel conducting his Bolero, a work which attained unexpected success. The composer had sketched it out merely as an experiment.

Ravel at the piano in 1933 at his home, Belvedère, at Montfort l'Anvaury. He died shortly after this picture was taken.

Enrique Granados put into music his impressions of Goya's art.

Isaac Albéniz. His Iberia evokes the atmosphere of Spain's colorful provinces.

Falla's ballet, The Three Cornered Hat, *was produced by Diaghilev in London in 1919, with stage designs by Pablo Picasso. (Paul Rosenberg Gallery)*

Impressionism in Spain and Italy

The attraction to exotic subjects and musical styles — medieval, Spanish, or oriental — was characteristic of the Romantic movement. Bizet first made extensive use of Spanish elements in his *Carmen,* and Debussy *(Iberia),* Chabrier *(España),* Ravel *(Rhapsodie Espagnole)* and others followed suit. In these composers, however, Spanish element meant local color rather than a *rapprochement* to any really Spanish school of music.

On the other hand, Manuel de Falla (1876–1946) combined a deeply Spanish musical personality with an eminently versatile European technique of composition. At the age of twenty-nine, Falla won recognition with his opera *La Vida Breve.* This is authentic Spanish music, based on the warm and passionate folk art of Andalusia; yet Falla — like Dvořák and Sibelius — is almost always able to be his own melodist. Falla took up residence in Paris, met Debussy, Ravel, and Dukas, and acquired the French school's refined and sophisticated musical language and technique.

Manuel de Falla (left) and the choreographer Massine in the courtyard of the Alhambra. Falla expressed the Spanish spirit and mood most eloquently in Nights in the Gardens of Spain, *a suite of three nocturnes for piano and orchestra.*

*El Amor Brujo (Love, the Magician;
1915)* a ballet with songs which became
popular all over the world demonstrates his
mastery of European technique. Thus while
a profoundly Spanish musician, at the same
time Falla must be regarded as an eminently
European composer in the mainstream of
Impressionism. His ties with the Spanish
past remained strong. In his keyboard music
there are many echoes of harpsichord and
guitar, while in *El Retablo de Maese Pedro,*
a delightful marionette play with singers,
the old Spanish dramatized *villancico* is recreated.

*Manuel de Falla, though befriended by men
like Albéniz, Debussy, and Ravel, was a
solitary, ascetic figure.*

*Ottorino Respighi. He wrote symphonic mu-
sic in a country dedicated to opera. His two
symphonic poems* The Fountains of Rome
(1916) and Pines of Rome *(1924) are elegant
evocations of the eternal city during different hours of the day.*

England's New Voices

DURING THE FIRST TWO decades of the 20th century English music reverberated with echoes of French impressionism. Besides pleasant, though somewhat eclectic composers like Frederick Delius (1862–1934) and Cyril Scott (1879–   ) the British Isles produced one musician of stature: Ralph Vaughan Williams.

Delius, of German parentage (the program of his first London concert in 1899 lists him as "Fritz" Delius), spent all his mature life outside of Britain; he made extended visits to Scandinavia, spent some time in Florida, where he was an unsuccessful citrus grower, and mainly lived in France. The decisive influences in his life were Grieg's music, and the music of the French Impressionists. Nevertheless, he shows an original musical mind quite removed from classical and traditional precepts. Confined for years to a wheelchair and suffering from blindness as well, this heroic composer, like Milton, continued his creative activity by dictating his scores to devoted friends.

Cyril Scott was also a product of German conservatories; he composed evocative piano pieces which had a vogue at the beginning of the 1900's.

The 20th century was well advanced before these cosmopolitan musicians gave way to truly British composers taking their nourishment from the national soil. This soil was largely cultivated by an able student of British folk music, Cecil Sharp, who spent his entire life collecting and publishing it. Acquaintance with his discoveries soon made the younger British composers realize that the folk song of their native land supplied impressions and models quite different from the German patterns that had furnished the point of departure for their elders. Through English folk song they were awakened to the genuine rhythm and inflections of the English language, which in turn led them to a true English melody. Then their attention turned to the incomparable art music of the Elizabethans and to Purcell's sturdy and unmistakably English musical diction. This influence became decisive for the future. The road from Renaissance polyphony and Baroque choral music to modern symphony was difficult, and not traveled by any continental composer; but after many trials, these fine musicians succeeded in finding their way.

Gustav Holst (1874–1934) was still only partly English. This is not merely because he had a Swedish father and an English mother (he dropped a "von" after 1914), but also because his works are a combination of genuinely English and exotic elements. His *The Planets* (1914–1916), an orchestral work with astrological and mystical themes, is still popular in England.

Delius in his summer house at Grez-sur-Loing, France.

The real master appeared finally in Ralph Vaughan Williams (1872–1958); in him the Parry-Stanford school produced a British musician who was an outstanding figure not only at home but in the world community of music. His *Fantasia on a Theme by Tallis* tells the story of his artistic descent. Vaughan Williams was a highly cultivated musician blessed with an inquisitive mind. He studied the works of his times, from Ravel to Sibelius, reacting to many stimuli and developing redoubtable and resourceful technical skills in the craft of composition, but these outside influences affected neither the roots nor the branches of his British musical heritage. He was a composer who never adhered to any style beyond the work in which he was engaged for the moment. Every one of his fine symphonies — he wrote nine — is different from the preceding one in style and tone. A prolific composer, he cultivated all fields of music with felicity. It is remarkable that the composer of the harsh, wild, and powerful Symphony in F Minor should also have created the ineffably gentle and idiomatic songs.

Benjamin Britten (1913–) is the most successful of the younger British composers — at any rate, he is the one best known abroad. A knowledgeable critic, Gerald Abraham, once called him "the Saint-Saëns of Britain." There is a good deal of truth in this judgment, for Britten is eclectic, able and fluent, technically versatile, and lacking in real depth. Essentially he is a more individual composer than Saint-Saëns; when he is really possessed by an idea, he can attain a fine lyric expression; at other times it is his technical fluency that carries the day.

Britten is best known for his operas, which have been well received everywhere. *Peter Grimes, Albert Herring,* and *The Rape of Lucretia* renewed English faith in opera and created a public for the modern lyric stage in England.

As we look at contemporary British music we see that the somewhat self-conscious attempt to create a specifically national style has gone; the English quality in this music is natural, and the composers after the mature Vaughan Williams could afford contact with European trends and could accept them without in the least compromising their patrimony.

Benjamin Britten. Through the work of this versatile composer, English music gained new distinction in the field of opera.

Ralph Vaughan Williams going over a score with Sir John Barbarolli. Although Vaughan Williams studied with Ravel, he was too much of an individualist to follow any school.

Book Eight

Soudeikine: Les Noces

TWENTIETH·CENTURY

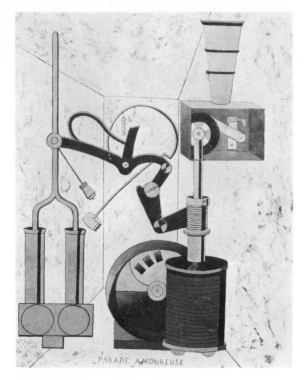

The fine arts sought to make contact with a civilization that glorified the machine. Music began to utilize sounds reminiscent of the throbbing of valves and pounding of pistons.

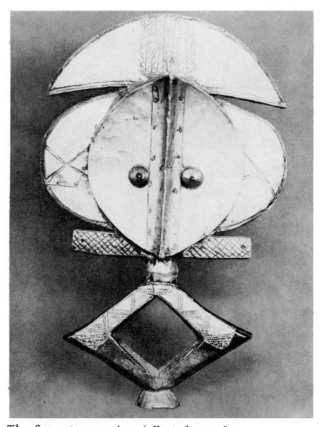

The fine arts were forcefully influenced in the 1920's by African sculpture. Similarly, contemporary musicians discovered African rhythms and the ecclesiastical modes, and used them as elements of the modern tonal language.

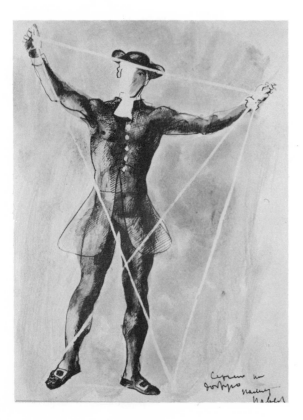

Music, like the ballet of the 1920's, stressed rhythm, a well-ordered physicality as a surcease for shattered nerves. Stravinsky renounced melody and proclaimed rhythm and motion the foundation of musical art. (Tschelitchev design for the ballet Ode).

Modern Music and Modern Life

THE 19TH CENTURY reached its end, after a long period of peace, in the atmosphere of an international cosmopolitan civilization; and every one was tired and bored with the large gestures, the always elevated tone, the eternal proclamations and apocalypses. 20th-century music began in this atmosphere of satiated stuffiness, but during the first four decades of the century the pace gradually quickened and, in a compressed fashion, the picture somewhat resembled the events which occurred between 1580 and 1660. First came revolutionary dissolution, then severe and tradition-respecting concentration. The boundary line between these two attitudes can be placed at around 1920–25, that is shortly after the death of Debussy and the end of the First World War. Before this date we witness dissolution, overpowering subjectivity, loose and uncertain forms, chromatically minced and crippled melody, decomposed tonality, Mahlerian verbosity. After it, there is a studied impersonality, form triumphantly hardened — in fact, ossified — wider, diatonic melodic lines, a new and tighter tonality, and an avariciously concise style of musical speech. After the early expansion came a stern contraction, somewhat analogous to the way in which Baroque Romanticism was followed by Baroque Classicism. But while there is much that is similar between the first halves of our century and of the 17th, the differences are more glaring — and not flattering to us.

The most prominent difference is social: the modern composer has lost his connection with the public and works in a vacuum. There are more orchestras and more opera houses than ever before, yet all this does not help the composer, for the crowds that attend the performances are no longer his. Mozart's *The Magic Flute* was immediately performed in a theater illuminated by oil lamps, and a couple of years later made the rounds of European stages; but Berg's *Wozzeck*, an acknowledged masterpiece of our century, waited for over three decades before it reached the electric footlights of the Metropolitan Opera House in New York. We must reckon with the masses, say the sociologists, because the future is theirs; but the masses have succumbed to the entertainment industry and to commercial music, things unknown a hundred years ago. There is another social factor, of course, which mitigates the gulf between composer and public; the gradual rise in musical literacy, the wide availability of good musical education; and this will, in due time, furnish a counterbalance to commercial music.

Challengers of Traditional Tonality:
Arnold Schoenberg and His School

In the music of the first half of the 20th century, everything around the chaotic circle of Arnold Schoenberg (1874–1951) seems calm and orderly — for Schoenberg and his school represent the first real break from the legacy of the long 19th century. The conventional symbols disappear in Schoenberg's music; we feel an imaginary glossary is necessary to follow the proceedings. Yet our objections are stilled if we view Schoenberg against the perspective of the thousand years of the history of Western music. Then the chaotic Schoenberg appears as a purposeful artist full of energy who created a new concept of musical space.

The deterioration of the post-Romantic music was due to several causes, of which the reaching of a stylistic impasse was decisive. Music no longer was developing toward a new style; musicians sought only to use the existing apparatus with more and more individual virtuosity. In an era of extreme individualism collective values cannot be established and preserved — and consequently music exhausts itself.

Schoenberg himself arrived at this extremity with his post-Romantic *Gurrelieder*, for voices and orchestra, after which all he could do was to swing boldly to a new point of departure. But before Schoenberg, a highly cultivated musician with a searching mind, became convinced of the necessity for

an absolutely fresh start, he tried to compromise. His position was not different from that of other musicians caught in the same dilemma. He too had inherited a lavish knowledge of the metier — but also a disordered situation. He tried very hard to solve the problem of what to do with his heritage, but he could not; *Verklärte Nacht,* and *Hängende Gärten* are the results of his attempt at reconciliation with Impressionism. Since this earnest and honest artist was not satisfied, he chose an altogether new road. That is why his mature art is so incredibly paradoxical and yet altogether logical and true.

Schoenberg's innovation, although naturally not entirely of his own devising, is the greatest single event in the music of the first half of the 20th century; and although it has the earmarks of a transitional phenomenon, it is quite possible that the second half will be dominated by it. After 1925, the thematic material in his works is based on a use of all twelve notes in the octave arranged in a certain order. This arrange-

Schoenberg as a teacher. After Hitler came to power, Schoenberg escaped to America and became professor of composition at the University of California in Los Angeles.

218

ment of the twelve notes — called the *tone-row* — is the theme, which is then developed with the aid of the most involved contrapuntal artifices. The row or series permits innumerable permutations in the order in which the twelve notes are arranged; nor does the involved canonic technique necessarily mean a curtailment of imagination. Furthermore, much highly emotional and expressive twelve-tone music has been and is being composed by distinguished musicians the world over. On the other hand, it must be admitted that in the hands of fanatics and imitators the texture of this music can become forbidding.

Among the immediate disciples of Schoenberg the outstanding were Anton von Webern (1883–1945), and Alban Berg (1885–1935). As can be seen, both of them died before their master, Webern under tragic circumstances — shot by an American sentry of the army of occupation. Webern was a musician with an exceedingly sensitive nervous system who immersed himself in contemplation and avoided the life around him. At times one has the distinct feeling that the composer might have been afraid of the reality of the sound of music. Webern wrote with a wholly admirable terse precision. He did not compose much and all of his pieces are brief, some of them lasting only a few seconds; but every one is a cameo. The world has been slow to comprehend the utter refinement of Webern's art; nonetheless his influence on musicians is pervasive and constantly increasing.

Alban Berg, like most other composers born toward the end of the 19th century, began writing music which echoed *Tristan*. A certain nervously animated rhythm, which is very characteristic of his music, was already present before he came under the influence of Schoenberg and espoused free tonality. Berg became a firm partisan of musical Expressionism and the movement's finest monument is his opera, *Wozzeck* (first integral performance, 1926). The libretto was Georg Büchner's (1813–1837) Romantic drama (1836); the German playwright's feverish scenes, his revolutionary spirit, sincere humanity, and pitiless psychological insight were akin to Berg's feelings.

Anton von Webern. His over-refined lonely lyricism blooms in an atmosphere of suffering isolation. His pieces are brief, often lasting only a few seconds, and have the quality of cameos.

Alban Berg shown with the portrait that Schoenberg, his teacher, painted of him. Like von Webern, Berg seemed to be detached from reality. When composing he would lock himself in his darkened room with windows closed even in summer.

Igor Stravinsky: From Exoticism to Classicism

A scene from Firebird: *The first performance of this Diaghilev ballet on June 25, 1910 in Paris marked the emergence of Stravinsky as a professional musician.*

Igor Stravinsky (1882–   ) started his career like every young Russian of the end of the century — in the shadow of Rimsky-Korsakov. His earlier works did not create particular interest, although they exhibit an astounding capacity for growth. Then in 1909, he met Serge Diaghilev, the famous impresario of the Ballet Russe; their collaboration proved to be most fruitful. The next ten years were devoted mainly to stage works: in 1910, the first performance of *The Firebird*, in 1912 *Petrushka,* in 1913 *The Rite of Spring.* The effeminate Impressionists were not prepared for such elemental power, such vigorous and blazing colors, and were amazed that a musician from remote Russia who sang of the glories of pagan rites could handle their musical language and their orchestra with a skill that none of them could match. The rank and file were scandalized — but the younger musicians instantly saw that this pagan music could lead them to their salvation and Stravinsky became their idol and master. The Russian master renounced his homeland and settled in Paris, and a curious process of acclimatization began. The semi-oriental visitor from Russia, still wearing a tunic, boots, and a fur cap, who wrote *The Rite of Spring* is transformed into a Parisian boulevardier in a dinner jacket, patent leather pumps, and a top hat, writing *Capriccio.* After the opera *Mavra* (1922), Stravinsky never again used a Russian subject.

A sketch made in 1921 by Stravinsky of Serge Diaghilev.

Stravinsky with Debussy in 1912. They met at the première of Firebird.

A drawing by Jean Cocteau of Stravinsky during the rehearsal for the Rite of Spring. The first performance of this piece in Paris in 1913 caused a scandal

Picasso's titlepage for Stravinsky's Ragtime (1918).

Stravinsky with Nijinsky, who created the role of Petrushka.

Benois's stagesetting for Petrushka, revived at Covent Garden. Stravinsky originally had planned the music for a puppet play. At Diaghilev's suggestion he transformed it into a ballet, a perfect vehicle for Nijinsky.

Figures by Picasso for Pulcinella, *a one-act ballet based on Pergolesi. This work marks Stravinsky's break with Russian emotionalism.*

Stravinsky's first major dramatic venture was Oedipus Rex *(1927).*

Stravinsky's earlier Russian music is full of rich color, good tunes, nerve-tingling rhythms, and Slavic abandon. It is dynamic music, always on the go, and infectiously attractive. But as Stravinsky became a champion of the music of the West, little if any Russian was left in him. He battled for neo-Classicism, joined the movement called "Back to Bach," and led an entirely new school and style which exerted an irresistible attraction upon musicians all over the world. The piano concerto (1924), piano sonata, and especially the scenic oratorio *Oedipus Rex* (1927), the ballet *Apollon Musagète* (*Apollo, Leader of the Muses,* 1928) are breathtaking in musicianship; but Stravinsky was unwilling to endow his prodigious musicianship with warmth and depth: he classicizes and archaizes. No Latin or Germanic composer, born to western Classicism, had ever dreamed of such an abstraction in the realm of the purely esthetic. Everything is austere, severe, absolutely stylized, impeccably built, but rather static, despite the glittering idiom. Yet only a few years later this enigmatic composer produced the *Sym-*

Igor Stravinsky in his home in Paris in the early 1920's. He was turning from the opulence of the Russian school to the workmanlike restraint of 18th-century classicism.

222

Stravinsky rehearsing. A small, wiry, and energetic man, Stravinsky, now in his seventies, continues to amaze the world. His most recent choral works, Canticum Sacrum *and* Threni, *were received with great respect.*

Stravinsky in Venice in 1956 at the première of Canticum Sacrum, *dedicated to Saint Mark.*

A scene from the première of Stravinsky's opera The Rake's Progress *at Venice in 1956.*

phony of Psalms, fresh in invention and profoundly moving in mood. In 1939 Stravinsky left France and settled in the United States, subsequently becoming an American citizen. The intervening years saw the appearance of many works, although few were of real significance, until 1951, when he produced his opera. *The Rake's Progress,* after the celebrated set of engravings by Hogarth, another unquestioned masterpiece. This remarkable and attractive work indicated one more stylistic departure, for the composer was using elements of French and Italian 18th-century comic opera; but still another conversion was to come. In *Canticum Sacrum,* and especially *Threni,* two choral-orchestral works of severe religious tone, Stravinsky has espoused dodecaphony, thus completely renouncing his past and burning all bridges behind him.

Both his character and historical position make Stravinsky a symbol of the cultural aspirations and disappointments of Russia, of its great power and of its failures. The struggle between East and West is exemplified in this great Russian master whose original elemental force was sacrificed to the blandishments of the ultra-cultivated West. The Eastern musician became the apostle of Western music, on which his influence has been and will continue to be tremendous; however, what really affected us was the earlier, uninhibited Russian master.

Béla Bartók in his home, playing a hurdy-gurdy. Bartók used elements from his country's music to revitalize the broad stream of Western music.

Béla Bartók: Passionate Dualist

Béla Bartók (1881–1945) came from an intelligent, music-loving, provincial middle-class family, his father being a teacher in an agricultural school. As a student at the Royal Academy of Music in Budapest, his work was inevitably that of a Central European dominated by Germanic influence, and his first models were Liszt, Wagner, and Strauss. But his discovery at an early stage of his development of the true folk music of the Hungarian peasants (as opposed to the Gypsy music that Schubert, Liszt, and Brahms made famous under the "Hungarian" label) changed the entire course of his life. It is no accident that the utilization of folkloristic material in art music, a trend typical of the earlier 20th century, was especially notable in southeastern Europe and in Russia. The mainstream of Western music did not flow through these countries, and they were ignorant of their true folk art. The discovery of genuine folk music proved to be of momentous importance for the development of 20th century music, for it enabled those regions to cast away the German and French influence and find their own individual way into the current of Western music. Obviously, the danger of using this vast treasure of music as mere exotic spice in an otherwise entirely

Bartók supervising the recording of a folk song in a Hungarian peasant village.

Western idiom was ever present, and many an excellent composer succumbed to it.

Bartók's great achievement was that instead of merely quoting the echoes of the past, he *absorbed* the past; and then, with firm conviction and with profound artistic faith, worked for the future. Through his original artistic personality the unspoiled energies of eastern European music burst upon the Western world with unparalleled intensity. He was a Western composer in the fullest sense, and what made him that was the passionate dualism in his work, the struggle of a highly trained, disciplined, and most accomplished occidental musical mind with the naïve, popular, oriental European heritage. The result was a personal dynamism, startling but also captivating.

It was only some time after his death, however, that the world began to realize that the barbaric vigor of his music, the slashing and infinitely complicated rhythms, the curiously haunting melodies, were not the sum total of Bartók's art. Beyond these were the uncompromising artistic integrity, fierce individualism, creative will, and noble humanity of his music. It is not only Hungarian music, it rises above all limitations and conventions to become one of the strongest voices of the 20th century. Nor does the presence of East European folk music explain Bartók's art; for in some of his greatest works, such as the string quartets or *Music for Strings, Percussion, and Celesta,* folk music has a minor role. What gives this music its tremendous dynamic tension is his incomparably original rhythmic sense, which is capable of demonic force.

In his younger years Bartók was a virtuoso pianist, a fact well demonstrated by his many fine piano compositions. Among these, his *Mikrokosmos* is a unique compendium of the art of piano playing. The 153 pieces are arranged in progressively difficult order and offer an endless variety of moods and technical problems. The concertos for piano, violin, and viola, as well as the extraordinary concerto for orchestra, are among the finest in the modern literature, while the six string quartets represent a body of chamber music comparable only to Beethoven's last works in this genre.

Bartók's art is expansive and eruptive, yet at the same time it is severe and secretive; far removed from any sentimentality, it is nonetheless filled with profound humanism. This great composer was in addition a fine musicologist, whose researches in folk music gave a new scope and new techniques to musical ethnology.

Bartók in America with the violinist Rudolph Kolisch during a rehearsal of his Music for Strings, Percussion and Celesta.

Bartók was a famous concert pianist; this explains why he wrote many of his most original pieces for the piano.

The group of French composers, who banded together in 1916 to form Les Six. With Jean Cocteau (at the piano) as their spokesman, they were (from left right): Darius Milhaud, Georges Auric, Arthur Honegger, Germaine Tailleferre, Francis Poulenc, Louis Durey.

Les Six: The Modern French Masters

AN ART AS pronouncedly individual as Debussy's will inevitably smother lesser contemporaries and successors, who in their helplessness will eventually turn against it. This is what happened when at about the time of Debussy's death the group *Les Six* was formed by Louis Durey, Darius Milhaud, Germaine Tailleferre, Georges Auric, Arthur Honegger, and Francis Poulenc. The group was not a real school, for each of these musicians went his own way; nevertheless their relationship was never disavowed. Their spiritual father was none other than Erik Satie, the erstwhile apostle of Debussy turned anti-Impressionist.

Of the Six, Arthur Honegger (1892–1955) and Darius Milhaud (1892–   ) achieved international popularity. In Honegger's music German and French elements are fused, unlike Milhaud's, which is entirely French; the reconciliation of these two elements give Honegger's work a stylistic individuality. A musician of strength and imagination, his talent is more illustrative and dramatic than lyric. An excellent contrapuntist and orchestrator, he rises above his French colleagues with the spaciousness of his concepts, which found scope in his fine symphonies, the Third and Fifth being especially notable. Honegger's fame

Arthur Honegger, Swiss by birth, was nevertheless a member of the modern French school. His Pacific 231 is the apotheosis of a locomotive.

Francis Poulenc at his chateau in Provence.

Darius Milhaud, a self-portrait done shortly after his arrival in the United States.

began with his symphonic studies *Pacific 231* (1923) and *Rugby* (1928); but he soon abandoned these post-Straussian tone poems as unworkable. His oratorio *King David* (1921) called attention to his best qualities, also present in the realistic lyric tragedy, *Antigone* (1927), and more recently in *Joan of Arc*.

Poulenc (1899–) and Georges Auric (1899–) took a path divergent from Honegger's; they wanted to please and entertain, something they could do with great ease. Auric's style is rather dry and cold, conspicuously lacking in melodic value, but Poulenc's music is fresh, urbane, elegant, and full of good melodies. He has a remarkable ability to transform prose into musical declamation; but this faultless musical declamation remains prose and seldom rises to the level of dramatic poetry. Nor is his music free of frivolity. This comment is not made on the basis of the delightfully bawdy irresponsibility of such a work as *Les Mammelles de Tiresias*, for the serious and religious *Dialogues of the Carmelites* has the same kind of music. It is Poulenc's fluency, his scented melodies, that make him an amiable and resourceful hedonist.

A poster for the first performance of Honegger's dramatic oratorio, King David, *done at Mézières, June 11, 1921. Written within two months,* King David *has become Honegger's best-known work.*

227

Paul Hindemith as a young violist shortly after the end of World War I. His experience as an ensemble player and soloist is reflected in his craftsmanlike music.

Ernst Krenek, another member of the advanced German school which included Hindemith, Toch, and Eissler. His jazz opera Jonny Strikes Up *had a considerable vogue in the 1920's.*

Paul Hindemith: A Leader of Contemporary Music

THE POLITICAL EVENTS in post-World War I Germany precluded an orderly development of the arts in the decades when the definitive lines of 20th-century music were being formulated. Then, during the Nazi regime, the war, and the immediate post-war era, German music, politically supervised for too long a time, lost contact with the international world. Some able musicians escaped the stifling atmosphere, and one of them, Paul Hindemith (1895–   ) who found refuge in the United States, became one of the leaders of contemporary music. Indeed, all aspirations of newer German music coalesced in this many-sided and phenomenally erudite composer, endowed with great facility and productivity. Hindemith is one of the few distinguished composers of modern times who is also an excellent executant — first a violinist and later a violist. His career as a composer bears a certain resemblance to Stravinsky's, for he too went through radical changes in style rather than following a straight line of development. This stamps him as a man of the day who has always concentrated on the prevailing tendencies; however, he does not compromise, nor is he a victim of manner-

Titlepage of Piano Suite *(1922) with Hindemith's own illustration. The composer has written musical interpretations of events and contemporary moods.*

228

Spielmusik: *Hindemith's interest has always centered around music playable by small groups. He is shown here conducting an orchestra of young people.*

isms. True to the everchanging intellectual climate in post-war Germany, some of his earlier works exhibit a dry linearity and acerbic satire *(Neues vom Tage,* 1929), but he can be very poetic, as in the fine song cycle *Das Marienleben,* or in the viola concerto *Der Schwanendreher* (1935). He also showed a passing interest in the movement called *Gebrauchsmusik,* i.e., workaday music, and in music for the home *(Hausmusik),* both of which invite the participation of dilettantes. Then came a neo-Classic phase, the revival of Baroque, polyphonically oriented textures. Today, Hindemith composes in a style that makes use of all modern techniques, tonal or atonal, except dodecaphony, to which he is opposed in principle.

One would think that all this would lead to eclecticism; but although sheer invention is perhaps not Hindemith's strongest quality, his mastery of the craft of composition is such that he can always assert his unmistakable individuality no matter what the medium. On the other hand, the frequent recasting of older works shows a certain restlessness, perhaps even hesitation.

Hindemith is a profound student of music whose musicological knowledge is considerable. Extremely prolific, he has composed in all departments of music, from the magnificent opera, *Mathis der Maler (Mathis the Painter),* to *Ludus Tonalis,* a versatile and varied modern counterpart to the *Well-Tempered Clavier.*

Hindemith in the 1930's, when he was compelled to leave Germany. He settled in America in 1939 and taught at the Yale School of Music. He now lives in Switzerland.

229

Serge Prokofiev as a boy of 10. His musical talent was first developed by his mother, a gifted pianist.

Prokofiev in 1917, the year he left Russia after composing the Scythian Suite *and* Classical Symphony.

Prokofiev (center) settled in Paris in 1923, joining the great impresario Diaghilev (standing).

Soviet Composers: Socialist Realism

AFTER THE 1917 REVOLUTION, great changes took place in Russian music. Many of the most talented composers emigrated, never to return, while those who stayed at home had to submit to official doctrines of proletarian aesthetics. For a while these men maintained their independence and even visited in the West, but after the Second World War conformity was ruthlessly enforced. Among the post-revolutionary musicians the outstanding figure is Sergei Prokofiev (1891–1953) — outstanding not only in Russian music, but in the music of the world. The amateurish quality of the work of many is entirely missing in Prokofiev. His music is utterly professional, showing French and even American influences, but always remaining distinctly personal and Russian. This music is light and pliable, elegant and transparent; it exhibits a pleasing, half-serious, rhetorical eloquence and a wonderful sense of irony and persiflage: his *Classical Symphony,* for example, and his opera, *The Love of Three Oranges.* Toward the end of his life this freshness and originality, expressed in fine concertos, symphonies, and sonatas, was finally destroyed by the pressure of Soviet art politics, and the composer of the opera *War and Peace* appears as a broken man.

Prokofiev shown after his return to Russia, where his modernism came under attack.

The Prince from The Love of Three Oranges, *premièred in Chicago in 1921.*

Katerina and her lover Sergei, a scene from Lady Macbeth of Mzensk, *banned by Stalin in 1936.*

Shostakovitch at the time of his first operatic venture The Nose, *based on a story by Gogol.*

At least Prokofiev succumbed only after producing a number of masterworks; but the leading Russian composer of the present, Dmitri Shostakovitch (1906–   ), who made a brilliant debut with his first symphony at the age of eighteen, was cut down in the flower of his creative life. This gifted composer tried to establish contact with the mainstream of contemporary music, but whenever he produced something original, such as the opera *Lady Macbeth of Mzensk,* or the *Fourth Symphony,* he was bitterly assailed by the Russians as a representative of bourgeois decadence and a propagandist for foreign modernism. A man of apparently weak character (or perhaps simply a man with a desire to stay alive) Shostakovitch has since admitted his sins and promised to remain faithful to socialist realism. His rehabilitation came with the *Fifth Symphony* which his judges found acceptable. His *Seventh Symphony (Leningrad),* composed during the holocaust of the siege, was a triumph. It is not a good work, but it is exciting, and it has become one of the most popular contemporary works in the free world. In fact, Shostakovitch was one of the most popular contemporary composers in the 1940's, after which his vogue began to decline. His latest symphonies — the Eighth to the Eleventh — have been poorly received, and his obsequious surrender of his artistic integrity has alienated even those who saw in him the successor to Prokofiev.

Dmitri Shostakovitch: he writes in a contemporary style toned down to conform with Soviet ideology.

Contemporary American Music

DURING THE LAST GENERATION, American music began to change; and in our own time we discover that although it does not cease to inspire, Europe no longer commands; American music, no matter how restricted its European success, has increased importance. The reason for this is that American music has ceased to be a provincial art; it has thrown away its traditional self-consciousness and its healthy direction and unconventionality has become one of its greatest attractions. No longer does it ostentatiously exhibit its national character by offering Negro and Indian tunes with German harmonization.

In the music of the generation that came on the scene in the late twenties there was something more than romantic Americanism, something more than a new style; there was an implicit new view of art and life. These composers did not challenge the old order of MacDowell and Parker; they simply composed as if they were unconscious that the old New England Romantics had ever existed: the birth of an American music was at hand.

Between the two generations, the old Romantics and the new "Internationalists," there is a lost generation whose unsatisfied passions led them down curious byways of art and musical experience. Carl Ruggles (1876–) is an outstanding figure in this generation, which protested vigorously against the survival of a past period of impersonal Romantic imitation. Theirs was a brave and bold effort of no small interest; but in spite of their undeniable spirit and sincerity, their interest is largely historical, for the music they wrote was never likely to influence the coming generation. The tragedy of these valiant progressives was that they were too eager to break with tradition.

Americans in Paris, 1926, a group of young American composers in the home of Nadia Boulanger. From left to right: Virgil Thomson, Walter Piston, Herbert Elwell, and Aaron Copland.

Charles Ives. He pioneered in 20th-century music, and waited for forty years before being recognized as a composer of great originality and daring.

Nonetheless, there was one figure among them who not only became the symbol of an American composer, but has also gradually come to be recognized as an authentic master — Charles Ives (1874–1954). Ives was an extraordinary phenomenon. Caught between Europe and America, accusing yet worshiping his Yankee Americanism, he hid his great struggle until it was too late. Far from being a "primitive," as sentimental commentators describe him, Ives had an entirely modern, complex, and cultivated mind which conditions in America prevented from developing in an orderly and natural way. His works are filled with the most fantastic stylistic suggestions woven together without any regard to prevailing musical conditions. At times his music seems disorganized, but there is scarcely a page in his mature works in which one cannot find the most delicate stylistic solutions among a crazy quilt of the most astoundingly original ideas.

During the third decade of our century many young American composers journeyed to the Paris of Stravinsky and Picasso. They found there not only music that overwhelmed them, but also an exceptionally able teacher to initiate them into its mysteries: Nadia Boulanger. The old German orientation of American music had completely yielded to the new Paris-based neo-Classicism, of which Stravinsky was the undisputed leader; and this new generation of American composers remained immune — for the time being — both to the tradition-

Aaron Copland: in his earlier style he mixed folk elements and echoes of jazz.

bound polyphony of Hindemith and the Expressionism of Schoenberg and his circle. After the return of the voyagers, around 1930, we suddenly discover a genuine school of modern American composers.

Aaron Copland (1900–), Roger Sessions (1896–), and Roy Harris (1898–) were among the first to be acknowledged as the harbingers of a new era. Copland started his career — as did a number of others — by blending jazz elements into his symphonic music. This was understandable, and even Ravel and Stravinsky tried it. However, although the jazz gave a certain piquancy to their language, today it is this very element, originally thought of as the genuine American stamp, which seems a little monotonous, the tricky rhythms a little contrived. Copland experienced the stylistic metamorphoses undergone by Stravinsky, proceeding from neo-

Classicism to dodecaphonism, but his strong individuality has never been threatened. He is a fastidiously creative artist, full of ideas, and with a melodic turn entirely his own.

Roger Sessions addresses himself to his task with the care and integrity of the master musician, and his expression has the force which derives from the application of firmly held and clearly appreciated artistic views. His music is hard and sober. Mind and experience speak from it; it is always serious, it has power but also lyric feeling, and it shows a phenomenal mastery of the metier.

Roy Harris came on the scene like a whirlwind, a lusty composer bursting with vitality; and for a while he was the most frequently performed American composer. A work like his *Third Symphony* was original, well made, and zestful, and it promised even more. But somehow, he has failed to sustain his early momentum.

234

Roy Harris. He writes buoyant music which reflects the vastness of his native prairie.

Walter Piston (1894–   ) is the classicist in this younger group. His symphonies and concertos, as well as his chamber music, testify to a highly cultivated original musical personality who remains unperturbed by trends and reactions. He is a master of the large form, of euphonious sound, of a musical texture that is as engaging as it is accomplished in every detail.

Among the others of this generation, Randall Thompson (1899–   ) is the outstanding choral composer, and Quincy Porter (1897–   ) the composer of fine-grained chamber music. A group of able composers, somewhat to the right of center, includes Howard Hanson (1896–   ) whose romantically colored orchestral and choral works are solidly made, and Douglas Moore (1893–   ) one of our ablest opera composers, with a special gift for lyricism. Then there are the "Experimentalists," led by Henry Cowell (1897–   ) whose symphonies and other works disclose a restless, inventive, and ever-young spirit of adventure. A special place must be assigned to Wallingford Riegger (1885-1961). His birth date might indicate he belongs to a much older generation than the leaders of today, but not his music. Riegger is recognized as a major and very modern American composer.

In the years following the fascist up-

Roger Sessions, a superb craftsman. His influence on young American composers has been decisive.

235

heaval in Europe, many distinguished composers came to the United States. At one time we counted among our guests the flower of contemporary creative minds: Schoenberg, Stravinsky, Bartók, Hindemith, Milhaud, Krenek, Martinu, Toch, and many others. This influx was bound to exert considerable influence on the younger generation. It is a measure of the maturity of American music that this overwhelming artistic invasion did not stifle native music, but on the contrary accelerated its growth. American composers were secure enough in their own aims to pick and choose, accept and reject.

Of the younger American composers, Elliott Carter (1908–   ) has a marked individuality expressed in superbly constructed works. Compositions such as his

A scene from Douglas Moore's opera, The Ballad of Baby Doe: *Colorado's silver king, Horace Tabor, marries Baby Doe.*

Howard Hanson. As a composer, conductor, and educator, Hanson has devoted himself to the cause of American music.

Samuel Barber. His opera, Vanessa, *has had international acclaim. Barber's musical idiom is romantic.*

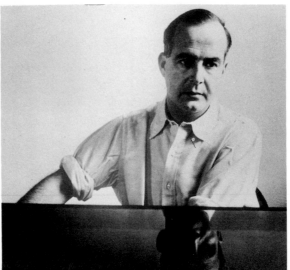

piano sonata and string quartet are in the front rank of contemporary music. William Schuman (1910-   ) has distinguished himself with powerful scores that have the long line, and can also sing. Again somewhat to right of center stands Samuel Barber (1910–   ) whose music attracts by its elegance and melodic finesse. But time passes, and this younger generation is being pressed by a youngest, teeming with talent. They are as yet too close to us to permit evaluation.

Finally, we turn to two outstanding composers, quite different in talent and personality. They are discussed together here, for neither fits easily into the orbit of American music, although both of them loom large on the contemporary scene. George Gershwin (1898–1937) is difficult to classify. If he is regarded only as a successful composer of semi-commercial music, one is in danger of undervaluing his very considerable gifts. On the other hand, as a composer of concertos and other symphonic works, his addiction to facile dance tunes and his primitive forms do not permit one to compare him with the distinguished masters of recent American music. Nevertheless, his position as a national musical hero is well-justified by his optimism, vitality, freshness of tone, and wholesome sentimentality, all of which reflect the American temperament. Gershwin was not satisfied with his artistic position, and he continually sought to improve his command of his metier, studying with various teachers to the end of his life. But it was difficult to break away from a life devoted to popular music. In his chef d'oeuvre, *Porgy and Bess*, which lies somewhere between opera and musical comedy, he wrote some extraordinarily intense lyric lines and achieved a powerful dramatic *espressivo*. We mourn the seemingly irreconcilable extremes of his peculiar talent, and critics often deplore his early death which precluded his more serious development from gaining the upper hand. But perhaps it is just this oscillation that made him what he is — a genuinely popular American composer.

A composer who more than any one else in this country contributed to public

Gershwin painting Arnold Schoenberg. All his life Gershwin admired the masters of serious music, Schoenberg, Stravinsky, and Ravel.

awareness of and understanding for contemporary opera, even opera as a form of art, is Gian Carlo Menotti. This is most remarkable because, although his successful operas treat either American subjects, or were written for America, the composer is not an American. Born in Italy in 1911, Menotti came to this country as a young man and studied at the Curtis Institute in Philadelphia. Making his home in the United States, although retaining his Italian citizenship, this very talented young man not only learned the national scene but also acquired such a fine command of English that he was able to write his own librettos. These are excellent vehicles for operas, and show the kind of flair for the lyric stage that only an Italian can possess. His style is neither revolutionary nor old-fashioned; he uses everything that suits the occasion, but the whole is dominated by a genuinely Italian gift for vocal writing. Menotti can be pastoral *(Amahl, and the Night Visitors,* the first successful television opera), and amusing *(The Telephone);* but he also sounds the accents of tragic conflict *(The Consul)* in a new form of verism that is entirely his own.

EPILOGUE

In the post-meridian of this century we are no longer sheltered and surrounded by a common and tractable form of life, by a rounded civilization, and by a more or less organized society. We live in the chaos of a disintegrating world whose substance is in the act of complete re-formation. The old has passed; the new, for some time faintly perceived, is in the process of crystallization. The phrase "decline of the West," uttered after the First World War, threatens to become a reality after the Second. We cling to our age-old civilization, but cannot be sure whether the point of gravity will not pass to other continents, whether what used to be western civilization may not become global, with fundamentally altered values.

At any rate, our situation signifies the end of a cultural epoch which until now was characteristic of the occident. It is indisputable that a radical change in the structure, order, and foundations of the world is occurring in which both material and spiritual matters demand a new approach and new attitude. This does not negate the future; yet the old plaint that music is finished, that no one can invent a melody any more, that what contemporary music offers is cacophony, is once more abroad. We have heard this complaint repeatedly throughout the history of music, and there is no reason to think that the situation is different now. The music with which we live is young, desperately young and vehement. But music is like nature, forever passing and renewing itself. The individual tree falls when its hour has come, but others grow in its place. Music too possesses eternal youth. And if, in a distant day, mankind's tired spirit may falter in its power to create, music will still throw a last light on the evening sky, for as it was the first artistic manifestation of man, it will be the last—as long as he remains human.

The highpoint in Gian Carlo Menotti's opera Amahl and the Night Visitors. *Amahl, a crippled boy, is miraculously cured when he offers his crutch to the three kings.*

ACKNOWLEDGMENTS

Grateful acknowledgment is due the following people for their suggestions and help in securing illustrations:

Dr. Victor Bator
Ralph L. Bergendahl
Robert Butts
Carlfranz Callies
Anselmo Carini
Mivana Coblentz
Aaron Copland
Dr. Eduard Crass
Guy Daniels
Ronald Eyer
Gerald Fitzgerald

Alfred V. Frankenstein
Roland Gelatt
Wilfried Goepel
Dr. M. Heiss
Bertha Himmler
Bruno Hoffmann
John Tasker Howard
Prof. A.J.B. Hutchings
Carlos Moseley
Mrs. Phillip Miller
Dr. Ernest Roth

Elly Schlee
Dr. Wolfgang Schmieder
Mrs. Gertrud Schoenberg
Janos Scholz
Brooks Shephard
Michael Sonino
William Speiser
Carl Stange
Gordon Stone
Virgil Thomson
Edward N. Waters

Sincere thanks are also due the Music Department of the New York Public Library, and the ever-helpful staff of the Library's Music Division; and the Music Departments of the Library of Congress, Columbia University, and Yale University.

SOURCE OF ILLUSTRATIONS

All illustrations, unless otherwise credited, are from *The Bettmann Archive, New York*.
The following individuals and organizations have kindly permitted the use of their material:

Adelys Photo: page 163 (top)
Akademie der Bildenden Kuenste Vienna,: 14-15
Archiv des Hauses Wahnfried: 132, 133
Artia: 185 (bottom right)
Beethoven Haus: 87 (top), 93 (top)
Berliner Staatsoper: 83 (top)
Boosey & Hawkes: 201 (center right), 214 (bottom right) 234
British Broadcasting Company: 122
British Information Service: 19 (center right)
Central City Opera House, Denver: 234 (center right)
Columbia University: 123 (top)
Deutsche Fotothek: 52 (bottom), 55 (bottom), 105 (top), 113 (center)
Eastman School of Music: 234 (center left)
Editions du Milieu de Monde: 206 (center; from *Ravel et Nous*)
Evans Brothers: 167 (top)
Finnish Information Service: 190 (top)
Fitzwilliam Museum: 55 (top)
G. D. Hackett: 237 (top right)
Historisches Museum der Stadt Wien: 95 (top), 120 (top left), 161 (top)
Bruno Hoffmann: 169 (top)
Houghton Mifflin: 220 (top left)
Internationale Gustave Mahler Gesellschaft: 194 (top)
Alfred A. Knopf: 213 (center)
Kurpfälzisches Museum: 111 (top)
Lifar Collection: 178 (center right), 216 (bottom right)
The Metropolitan Museum of Art: 61 (bottom right)

Musical America; 179 (top right), 201 (top left) National Portrait Gallery: 31 (center)
New York Times: 235
Oesterreichische Nationalbibliothek: 72 (bottom), 74 (bottom), 75 (bottom), 83 (bottom), 88, 89 (center), 93 (bottom), 100 (bottom), 142 (bottom), 144, 147 (top right, center left), 148 (top center), 195 (bottom), 196 (bottom)
Opera News: 202 (center right)
Oxford University Press: 232 (bottom left)
Fred Plaut: 223 (top left), 227 (top left), 235 (top right)
Polish Information Service: 116 (bottom), 117 (both)
Reger Archiv: 197
Ricordi Archiv: 153 (bottom), 155 (top right), 203 (top), 204 (top)
Helena Rubinstein Collection: 216 (center right)
Schumann Museum: 110 (top)
B. Schott's Söhne: 220 (bottom right), 228, 229
Sovfoto: 231 (bottom)
Stadtmuseum Salzburg: 76, 77 (top)
Stadt und Universitaetsbliothek Frankfurt: 198 (bottom)
Tate Gallery: 53 (bottom)
Tchaikovsky House and State Museum: 181 (center)
University of California: 218 (bottom right)
Roger Viollet: 206 (top right)
Richard Wagner Archiv: 130, 132
Roger Wild: 226 (bottom right)

INDEX